D0874083

BIBLE KEY WORDS

XI. LAW

In the same series

LOVE

THE CHURCH

SIN

RIGHTEOUSNESS

GNOSIS

APOSTLESHIP

BASILEIA

LORD

SPIRIT OF GOD

FAITH

In preparation

WRATH

LIFE and DEATH

HOPE

BIBLE KEY WORDS
FROM GERHARD KITTEL'S
*THEOLOGISCHES WÖRTERBUCH
ZUM NEUEN TESTAMENT*

LAW

BY

HERMANN KLEINKNECHT
and W. GUTBROD

ADAM & CHARLES BLACK
LONDON

FIRST PUBLISHED 1962
A. AND C. BLACK LIMITED
4, 5 AND 6 SOHO SQUARE, LONDON W.1

Translation from the German
by Dorothea M. Barton, M.A.
edited by P. R. Ackroyd, Ph.D.
© 1962 A. & C. Black Ltd

PRINTED IN GREAT BRITAIN BY
ROBERT CUNNINGHAM AND SONS LTD, ALVA

EDITOR'S PREFACE

THIS book is a translation of the article Νόμος in the *Theologisches Wörterbuch zum Neuen Testament* (TWNT), begun by G. Kittel and now edited by G. Friedrich, Vol. IV pp. 1016-1084, and written by Drs Kleinknecht and W. Gutbrod (1911-1941). Apart from some abbreviation in Chapter I and some curtailing of footnotes, the whole text is here translated. The retaining of references to many German works in an English translation may seem unnecessary to some readers. But while it is clear that those who read German easily will turn to the original rather than to a translation, there are many among those who read theological books who have a little German and who may wish to follow up a particular point without the labour of searching the original for an elusive reference. Nor does it seem altogether inappropriate that statements should be supported by the authority for them, since the weightiness or the bias of that authority may well influence the reader's judgement of what is here said.

The article on Law was published in 1942. Its text here is translated unchanged, but some additions have been made to the Bibliography and by way of footnotes. References to more recent works may be found in the newer Theologies of Old and New Testaments, and in other books to which reference has now been included. A special note may, however, be made here of a field of study entirely unavailable to the original authors, that of the Qumran documents. A fuller understanding of the background to the New Testament interpretation of Law will be one of the contributions which this new field may be expected to bring.

The reader may be referred to Millar Burrows, *New Light on the Dead Sea Scrolls* (1958), for much bibliographical information, and especially there to chapter XXXII.

The still common antithesis between Law and Gospel—narrowly interpreted—has tended to simplify in the minds of many the relationship between Old and New Testaments, and also that between Judaism and Christianity. Some parts of this present work may perhaps help to enlarge the understanding of the term Law as it appears in the Old Testament and in Judaism—and here the Qumran material may be able to fill in some of the gaps, and dialogue between Christians and Jews may also help to clarify the issues. The understanding of the nature of Law is a matter which vitally affects the understanding of the Gospel; and the relationship between Gospel and Law, Gospel and Ethic, is one in which clear and constructive thinking—related to sound exegesis of biblical material—is an ever present necessity.[1]

All Hebrew words have been transliterated and, where necessary, translated. Greek words are not transliterated. Where quotations are given from elsewhere than the New Testament (or Septuagint), a translation has been given, except where the meaning is evident or where the actual Greek word used is of particular importance. In a number of cases translations have been given of crucial Greek words, but these are to be taken only as rough guides to the meaning, since, as will appear from their contents, these are words which are deserving of full and separate study. Such of them as appear in the New Testament are, of course, so treated in other volumes of TWNT.

[1] Cf. G. A. F. Knight, *Law and Grace* (1962) for a fresh discussion of these issues.

CONTENTS

BIBLIOGRAPHY

CHAPTER I

In Plato's *Laws* (*Leges*) the reflexions on law and the concept of it which had developed during the course of history were expressed in an exalted form. Amongst the rich literature on νόμος, of which only a small part has been preserved, the following may be mentioned:

PSEUD.-PLATO: *Minos.*

PSEUD.-DEMOSTHENES: *Orationes* 25, 15 ff.

CHRYSIPPUS: fr. 314 ff. (III, pp. 77 ff. von Arnim).

CICERO: *De Legibus.*

DIO CHRYSOSTOM: *Orationes* 58 (Budé).

STOBAEUS: *Eclogae* IV.115-83.

Orphic Hymns (ed. W. Quandt, *Orphei Hymni* [²1955]), 64.

Modern Studies

U. VON MILAMOWITZ: 'Aus Kydathen, Excursus 1: Die Herrschaft des Gesetzes', PhU, 1 (1880), pp. 47 ff.

R. HIRZEL: *Themis, Dike und Verwandtes* (1907), pp. 133 ff.

—— '*ΑΓΡΑΦΟΣ ΝΟΜΟΣ*', *Abhandlungen Sächsische Akademie der Wissenschaften*, 20 (1900), pp. 65 ff.

V. EHRENBERG: *Die Rechtsidee im frühen Griechentum* (1921), pp. 103 ff.

W. JAEGER: 'Die griechische Staatsethik im Zeitalter des Plato' (1924), *Humanistische Reden und Vorträge* (1937), pp. 96 ff.

—— *Paideia* (1934), pp. 152 ff.

H. E. STIER: '*ΝΟΜΟΣ ΒΑΣΙΛΕΥΣ*', *Philol.*, 83 (1928), pp. 225 ff.

H. BOGNER: 'Der griechische Nomos. Die Zersetzung des griechischen Nomos', *Deutsches Volkstum*, 13 (1931), pp. 745ff., 854 ff.

M. MUHL: 'Untersuchungen zur altorientalischen und althellenischen Gesetzgebung', *Klio*, Beiheft 29 (1933), pp. 85 ff.

U. GALLI: *Platone e il Nomos* (1937).

A. BILL: *La morale et la loi dans la philosophie antique* (1928), especially pp. 261 ff., where the most important ancient texts for νόμος are brought together.

K. KERENYI, *Die antike Religion* (1940), pp. 77 ff.

Chapters II-IV

Reference may be made to the general Theologies of the Old and New Testaments

Chapter II

A. ALT: *Die Ursprünge des israelitischen Rechts* (1934), = *Kleine Schriften*, I (1953), pp. 278-332.

J. BEGRICH: 'Die priesterliche Thora', *Werden und Wesen des AT*, edited by Volz, Stummer, Hempel (1936), pp. 63 ff.

A. JEPSEN: *Untersuchungen zum Bundesbuch* (1927).

O. PROCKSCH: *Die Elohimquelle* (1906), pp. 225 ff., 263 ff.

L. KÖHLER: 'Der Dekalog', ThR (1929), pp. 161 ff.

G. VON RAD: *Das Gottesvolk im Deuteronomium* (1929).

H. H. SCHAEDER: *Esra der Schreiber* (1930).

J. B. PRITCHARD: *Ancient Near Eastern Texts* ([2]1955) for ancient legal texts.

Chapter III

BOUSSET-GRESSMANN = W. Bousset, *Die Religion des Judentums im späthellenistischen Zeitalter*, ed H. Gressmann ([3]1926).

M. NOTH: *Die Gesetze im Pentateuch* (1940), reprinted in *Gesammelte Studien zum AT* (1957), pp. 9-141.

G. ÖSTBORN: *Torah in the OT* (1945).

L. COUARD: *Die religiösen und sittlichen Anschauungen der alttestamentlichen Apokryphen und Pseudepigraphen* (1907).

S. KAATZ: *Die mündliche Lehre und ihr Dogma* (1921/22).

M. LÖWY: 'Die paulinische Lehre vom Gesetz', *Monatsschrift für Geschichte und Wissenschaft des Judentums* (1903 f.).

E. STEIN: *Die allegorische Exegese des Philo aus Alexandreia* (1929).

—— *Philo und der Midrasch* (1931).

J. WOHLGEMUTH: 'Das jüdische Religionsgesetz in jüdischer Beleuchtung', *Beilage zum Jahresbericht* (1918/19) *des Rabbinerseminars Berlin* (1919).

D. DAUBE: *Studies in Biblical Law* (1947).

G. F. MOORE: *Judaism* 3 vols. (1927-30).

Chapter IV

K. BENZ: 'Die Stellung Jesu zum alttestamentlichen Gesetz', *Biblische Studien*, XIX, 1 (1914).

W. BRANDT: *Das Gesetz Israels und die Gesetze der Heiden be Paulus und im Hebräerbrief* (1934).

B. H. BRANSCOMB: *Jesus and the law of Moses* (New York, 1930).

R. BULTMANN: 'Die Bedeutung des geschichtlichen Jesus für die Theologie des Paulus', *Glauben und Verstehen* (1933).

H. CREMER: *Biblisch theologisches Wörterbuch des nt.lichen Griechisch*, W. J. Kögel ([11]1923).

E. GRAFE: *Die paulinische Lehre vom Gesetz* ([2]1893).

A. HARNACK: 'Hat Jesus das alttestamentliche Gesetz abgeschafft?, *Aus Wissenschaft und Leben*, II (1911), pp. 225 ff.

J. HERKENRATH: *Die Ethik Jesu in ihren Grundzügen* (1926).

A. JUNCKER: *Die Ethik des Apostels Paulus*, I (1904), II (1919).

G. KITTEL: 'Die Stellung des Jakobus zu Judentum und Christentum', ZNW, 30 (1931), 145 ff.

E. LOHMEYER: *Grundlagen paulinischer Theologie* (1929), chapter I.

O. MICHEL: *Paulus und seine Bibel* (1929).

A. W. SLATEN: 'The qualitative use of "nomos" in the Pauline Epistles', *American Journal of Theology*, XXIII (1919), 213 ff.

E. BRUNNER: *Der Mensch im Widerspruch* (1937), pp. 150 ff., 532 ff. E.T. *Man in Revolt* (1939), pp. 155 ff., 516 f.

T. W. MANSON: *Ethics and the Gospel* (1960), esp. ch. III.

W. D. DAVIES: *Paul and Rabbinic Judaism* (1948), esp. ch. 7.

—— *Torah in the Messianic Age and for the Age to Come* (JBL Monograph Series VII, 1952).

D. DAUBE: *The NT and Rabbinic Judaism* (1956).

ABBREVIATIONS

BZAW	*Beihefte der Zeitschrift für die alttestamentliche Wissenschaft*
Diels	H. Diels, *Die Fragmente der Vorsokratiker*, ed. W. Kranz (I, [7]1954; II, III, [6]1952); cf. K. Freeman, *Ancilla to the PreSocratic Philosophers. A complete translation of the fragments in Diels* . . . (1948).
Ditt Or	W. Dittenberger, *Orientis Graeci Inscriptiones Selectae*, I-II (1903-5).
Ditt Syll	W. Dittenberger, *Sylloge Inscriptionum Graecarum*, I-IV, 1, 2 ([3]1915-24).
ET	English translation.
EVV	English versions.
IEJ	*Israel Exploration Journal.*
MGWJ	*Monatsschrift für Geschichte und Wissenschaft des Judentums.*
Philol	*Philologus, Zeitschrift für das klassische Altertum.*
PhU	*Philologische Untersuchungen.*
TGF	*Tragicorum Graecorum Fragmenta*, ed. A. Nauck ([2]1899).
ThR	*Theologische Rundschau.*
ThStKr	*Theologische Studien und Kritiken.*
TWNT	*Theologisches Wörterbuch zum Neuen Testament*, ed. G. Friedrich.
ZAW	*Zeitschrift für die alttestamentliche Wissenschaft.*
ZNW	*Zeitschrift für die neutestamentliche Wissenschaft.*

Works which appear in the Bibliography are referred to in the text and footnotes by the author's name either alone or with an abbreviated title. References to classical texts are in some cases followed by the name of the editor whose text has been used.

I. *ΝΟΜΟΣ* IN THE GREEK AND HELLENISTIC WORLD

1. *The meaning of the word* νόμος

(a) νόμος belongs by its etymology to νέμω, *deal out* or *dispense*, and corresponding to this it had in early times a comprehensive range of meaning as 'the characteristic quality which is dealt out to each one',[1] in so far as, in the first instance, this is understood in general to mean *every kind of existing or valid standard, order, practice, usage, custom*. νόμος is everything that is accepted and usual (cf. Pseud.-Plat. *Min.* 313b; cf. Aristoph. *Nu.* 1185 f., 1420 ff.; Xenoph. *Mem.* IV.4, 19). The concept is religious in origin and plays an important part in the cult. The connexion between νόμος and *worship of the gods* is expressed linguistically in the regular phrase νομίζειν θέους (Hdt. 1.131, 4.59; Aristoph. *Nu.* 329, 423), i.e. to honour the gods according to the cultic usage of the city-state by taking part in the (civic) public worship[2] (cf. Hes. fr. 221 (Rzach.), Plat. *Crat.* 400 e). νόμος covers such matters as marriage, procreation (Plat. *Leg.* IX.720 e ff.), love (Plat. *Symp.* 182 a), communal meals, schools for physical training,

---

[1] Walde-Pokorny 2 (1927), 330. Greek philosophy expounding the νόμος concept had special delight in alluding to this etymological origin (Plat. *Leg.* IV.714a; Pseud.-Plat. *Min.* 317d; M. Ant. 10.25; Plut. *Quaest. Conv.* 2.10 (II.644c)). This basic concept of νέμειν explains the fact that νόμος in the course of its development occurs with the meaning of 'connected by close kinship', and frequently as almost synonymous with or equivalent to *right* (cf. *Righteousness* in this series), *order, reason, mind*.

[2] So still in the formal accusation against Socrates (Xenoph. *Mem.* I.1.1 f.) νομίζειν is first transferred in Plat. *Apol.* 26c ff. to the intellectual meaning of *acknowledge, believe* (cf. Aristoph. *Nu.* 819; Eur. *Suppl.* 732). Cf. A. Menzel, *Hellenika* (1938), pp. 17 f.; J. Tate, *Class. Rev.* 51 (1937), pp. 3 ff.

the use of arms (Plat. *Leg.* I.625 c), above all the honouring and burial of the dead (Thuc. 2.35; Eur. *Suppl.* 563; Isoc. *Or.* 2.169). The arrangement and 'rules' for the Nemean games (Pind. *Nem.* 10.28, cf. *Isthm.* 2.38) can be designated νόμος just as easily as a political organisation and 'constitution' (Pind. *Pyth.* 2.86, 10.70). The gods too have νόμοι (Pind. *Pyth.* 2.43, *Nem.* 1.72; cf. Hes. *Theog.* 66). This wide use of the word has always been preserved.

(*b*) As the Greek world became organised politically, νόμος was used in addition especially in the sphere of the law and the state: the *judges' rule*, the *legal usage*, became a consciously settled and binding νόμος, the *law*. At the same time the political and the absolute law are not differentiated (Heracl. fr. 114 (I.176.5 ff. Diels[5]); Aesch. *Prom.* 150 f.; Pind. fr. 169; Soph. *Oed. Tyr.* 865). νόμος is expanded into the (divine) *universal law* (Plat. *Leg.* IV.716a; Callim. *Hymn* 5.100, M.Ant. 7.9), into the *'natural' law* (Plat. *Gorg.* 483 e; Dio Chrys. *Or.* 58.5 (Budé); Porphyr. *Abst.* 2.61), into the (philosophical) *moral law* (Epict. *Diss.* I.26.1; Muson. p. 87, 5 ff. (Hense)).

(*c*) Not until the fifth century, when we might say that the νόμος is written down in the individual νόμοι, does there arise in connexion with the development of democracy the particular meaning of *written law*, the *expression fixed in writing of the legal system and political constitution of the democratic city-state* (or *polis*) (Aristot. *Resp. Ath.* 7.1; Andoc. *Myst.* 83). Xenophon in *Mem.* I, 2, 42 ff. gives the definition of constitutional law: *Laws are all the rules approved and enacted by the majority in the assembly.* νόμος becomes the *compulsory order* and *command* by the state and punishment is involved if it is not obeyed (Antiphon *Or.* 6.4; Democr. fr. 181 (II.181.11 ff. Diels[5]); Pseud.-Aristot. *Rhet. Al.* 2p. 1422a, 2 ff.).

(d) When νόμος was understood in contrast to the divine nature (φύσις) essentially as a variable *human ordinance* (Hippocr. *Vict.* 1.11; Diod. S. Excerpta Vaticana 7.26 [p. 26 Dindorf 7], it could finally when used by the Sophists at the end of the fifth century acquire the debased meaning of a *contract* or an *agreement* (Aristoph. *Av.* 755 ff.); especially in the formula νόμῳ/φύσει (Democr. fr. 9 [II.139.10 ff.]; Hippias in Plat. *Prot.* 337c), a meaning which is by no means originally to be found in νόμος.

(e) The fundamental meaning of νόμος = *order* (τάξις) led in music to a technical term: *mode, manner of singing, melody, Nomos* (Alcman fr. 93 Diehl; Hom. *Hymn Ap.* 20; Aesch. *Prom.* 576). Since Plato the twofold meaning in politics and music of the 'mode of the law' was used again and again as a play on the word (Plat. *Leg.* IV.722d f.; 800a; Archytas Pythagoraeus in Stob. *Ecl.* IV.1.138 (p. 88, 2 ff. Hense); Max. Tyr. 6, 7).

If we have John vii.51 and Rom. iii.19 in view, it is not unimportant that νόμος too, like various other characteristic concepts of the Greek world, is personified and appears as a divine figure in poetry (Eur. *Hec.* 799 f.; Plat. *Crito* 50a ff.) and later in theology (Procl. in *Rem. Publ.* II.307.20 ff. (Kroll)). This is the place too for the expressions *the law regulates, declares, says* (Inscrip. Magn. 92a, 11; b 16; Plat. *Resp.* V.451b; Callim. *Hymn* 5.100)[1] as well as for the designation of the νόμος as δεσπότης (Hdt. 7.104), τύραννος (Plat. *Prot.* 337e), βασιλεύς[2] (Pind. fr. 169 *et passim*), and finally even as θεός (Plat. *Ep.* VIII.354e; TGF fr. adesp 471). Dio Chrys. (*Or.* 58.8 (Budé)) praises the νόμος in a mythical form as *actually the son of Zeus*. It

---

[1] cf. W. Schubart, 'Das Gesetz und der Kaiser in griech. Urkunden', *Klio* 30 (1937), pp. 56 ff.

[2] cf. *Basileia* in this series (1957).

occurs also in Orphism as assistant of Zeus (*Orph. Fr.* 160 (Kern)) with Δικαιοσύνη as the daughter of itself and of Εὐσέβεια (*Orph. Fr.* 159), and among the Orphic songs there is even a hymn addressed to law as a cosmic power (*Hymn Orph.* (ed. Quandt, 1941) 64).

2. *The nature and development of the* νόμος *concept in the Greek world*

νόμος was originally, before it was written down, rooted in religion as the embodiment of all that was valid in the affairs of the community. In the expressions τὰ νομιζόμενα, νομίζειν Θεούς (cf. p. 1) its relationship to the cult and to the worship of the gods has been permanently kept alive (cf. the Pythagorean precept in *Carmen Aureum* 1 f.; Jambl. *Vit. Pyth.* 144; (Diog. L.8.33)). Even the written νόμος in the city-state is considered to be the expression of the will of the deity who holds sway over the city (Aristot. *Pol.* 3.16, p. 1287a, 28 ff., cf. Plat. *Leg.* IV.712b). Its deep roots in the divine, which it always preserved, give to the Greek concept of νόμος its characteristic meaning and its real centre.

This is true particularly with reference to its origin: it is part of the nature of the νόμος to have an originator. Either it has been given by the gods, or it is the creation of a great personage, the lawgiver, one who is the kind of man gifted with understanding in a particularly high degree by the gods or of himself. By this means the νόμος becomes a work of the highest 'art' and wisdom. This does not prevent the laws, given to the people mythically or historically, from being often also traced back indirectly to particular gods or to the religious authority of Delphi. When finally the νόμοι in the city-state are brought about by mutual agreement and men's votes (Xenoph. *Mem.* I.2.42 f.), that is the beginning of their decline: soon they are no longer νόμοι, but only decrees (ψηφίσματα) (Demosth. *Or.* 20, 89 ff.).

(*a*) In the earliest period the νόμος as a creation and manifestation of Zeus βασιλεύς is firmly attached to a divine being who inspires belief.

Already myth refers the lawgiving of king Minos (βασιλεὺς καὶ νομοθέτης, Plut. *Thes.* 16 (I.7)) back to his association with Zeus (cf. Plat. *Leg.* I.624). The god is the original archetype of royal power and wisdom which express themselves in the νόμος. In Hesiod *Theogn.* 901 ff. the θεῶν βασιλεύς (886) after his victory over the Titans enters into a marriage with Themis, out of which springs in addition to Δίκη and Εἰρήνη, also Εὐνομίη, i.e. the 'correct order', the 'good νόμος'.[1] When Pindar in fr. 169 extols the νόμος as *monarch of mortal men and of the Immortals*, one who *leads on violence with a high hand dressing it as justice*, it can be recognised from the form of the wording as well as from the connexion of thought that here the νόμος occupies the position of him who is plainly the πάντων βασιλεύς (Democr. fr. 30 (II.151, 14 Diels⁵); Hes. fr. 195 (Rzach), cf. Theog. 923), and holds power and law together in his hand, namely Zeus.[2] He established the νόμος that the animals should devour each other by force (βία), but that mankind should live according to the δίκη which he gave them (Hes. *Op.* 276 ff.). The lawgiver Solon prided himself on the fact that he joined in marriage βία and δίκη (fr. 24.15 f. Diehl)

---

[1] Kingship and the establishment of εὐνομίη belonged in the early Greek world generally to a large extent together (cf. Hdt. 1.97 ff.; Plut. *Num.* 4); cf also Plato *Polit.* 300c/e).

[2] So now also K. Kerenyi, p. 78. For the history of Pindar's often quoted and misinterpreted saying (Hdt. 3.38; Anonym. Jambl. 6.1 (II.402.28 f. Diels⁵); Plat. *Gorg.* 484b, *Leg.* III.690b/c, IV.714c; Chrysipp. fr. 314 [III.77.34 ff. v. Arnim]) cf. H. E. Stier, pp. 225 ff.

by the power of law (κράτει νόμου), i.e. as a result of the complete power of such a *divine standard*, of a *determination for order* and of a personal *sense of what is right*— all this is involved in νόμος.

In accordance with its nature νόμος has developed into *justice*, as a result of its struggle for the right within the organisation of human life (Plut. *Princ. Inerud.* 3 (II.780e) cf. p. 1, no. 1). But *right* (δίκη) and also *reverence* (αἰδώς, expressed in the νόμος) rest with Zeus (Plat. *Prot.* 322d; Ael. Arist. *Or.* 43, 20 (344 Keil)); couched in terms which combine myth and religion: the goddess Dike in the retinue of the supreme ruler (βασιλεύς, Plut. *Exil.* 5 [II.601b]) keeps watch over the θεῖος νόμος (*Orph. Fr.* 21 (Kern); Plat. *Leg.* IV.716a). Thus νόμος always remained into the later ancient period linked in a special way with Zeus (cf. p. 3).

In the city-state the customs inherited from early days continued to develop into a permanent constitution and became the embodiment of all legal standards of what is right. At this point the concept reaches its characteristic elaboration and position of supremacy. For the state in its spiritual form is called by the Greeks νόμος (Aristot. of Demosth. in Stob. *Ecl.* IV.1.144 (p. 90 Hense); Aristot. *Pol.* 4.4, p. 1292a, 32). Therefore the people must fight for its νόμος as for its walls (Heracl. fr. 44 (I.160, 13 f. Diels⁵)). It is the sovereign power which as βασιλεύς or δεσπότης (cf. p. 14) gives orders in the city-state and so, for instance, bids the Spartans conquer or die in the battle (Hdt. 7.104).

(*b*) The new understanding of existence in the sixth century changes the content of νόμος correspondingly. It is not yet dissociated from the divine; now what was formerly Zeus is merely given a fresh form as the divine principle. The idea of the cosmos creates the idea that

the νόμος is an image of the universe in which the same
δίκη rules as in political life. Terrestrial law is only a
particular case of the divine law in the cosmos (Heracl.
fr. 114 (I.176.5 ff. Diels⁵)). Man is not able to exist
without the νόμος of his city-state, but he is even less
able to exist without the νόμος of the cosmos.

The Stoics, who based themselves upon Heraclitus,
later looked on this as the earliest form in which their
cosmopolitanism appeared (cf. Cleanthes fr. 537
(I.121.34 f. v. Arnim); Dio Chrys. *Or.* 58.2 (Budé)).
In contrast to this, Heraclitus maintains the sense of
being rooted in the concrete νόμος πόλεως. In fact
the laws of the state are such a 'strong' standard (cf.
fr. 44 (I.160.13 f. Diels⁵)) that Heraclitus uses them
as the basis from which to understand the universe:
the νόμος of the city-state is 'something held in common' (ξυνόν or κοινόν (common) Pseudo-Demosth.
Or. 25.15 f.[1]; cf. Plat. *Crito* 50a, *Leg.* I.645a; Plut.
Quaest. Conv. II.10.2 (II.644e, 7); i.e. in a life κατὰ
νόμον the citizen lives, as it were, the κοινὸς βίος in
contrast with the private existence of each individual.
Corresponding to this there is in the cosmos το ξυνὸν
πάντων which is explained by the image of the city-state
and its νόμος: it is the divine law of the universe which
must be grasped by the mind (νοῦς, ξὺν νόῳ) and
'followed' like the λόγος and the deity (fr. 2 [I.151.1 ff.
Diels⁵]). Perception means here perception of a
universal law and thus at the same time the performance of it. Both of these together are in Greek
φρονεῖν: for *the thinking faculty* (φρονέειν) *is common to all*
(fr. 113 (I.176.4 Diels⁵)); the ξυνόν is the law of the
universe.

(c) The problem raised by the existence of a νόμος
which is contrary to another νόμος (cf. Democr. fr. 259
(II.198.2 ff. Diels⁵)) and is therefore 'not unambigu-

[1] cf. M. Pohlenz in NGG (1924), pp. 19 ff.

ously clear',[1] and so the problem of whether it can be
carried out, dawned upon the Greeks for the first
time in tragedy. Whilst criticism of the νόμος was
opening up new aspects on every side in the most varied
forms (cf. p. 9 f.), Sophocles in the *Antigone* once more
lets 'the νόμος triumph in its double form'.[2] Although
the law of the state was founded originally on that of
the gods, yet in Antigone's speech in her defence
(450 ff.) an unwritten, divine law is set up against the
written law of the city-state: neither Zeus nor Δική
who *enacted not these human laws* (452) dictated her
action to Antigone, but the *immutable unwritten laws of
heaven* (459 f.).[3] There springs from an ancient source
above the law of the state and originating in the divine
world another law, equally divine. But where the law
originating with God can no longer be reconciled with
God, there arises the dilemma for the individual: the
tragic end of Antigone and the downfall of Creon.
Nothing is so characteristic of the way the Greek
understood human existence as the fact that when he
came up against that aspect of the law as a whole which
had a twofold interpretation and could not be carried
out (in so far as the performance of one part of it
necessarily involved the breach of another part), it
did not occur to him to recognise in himself the man
who is by nature utterly incapable of obeying the law.
He interprets the conflict which caused Antigone to
perish as the eternal tragic conflict of a law originating
with God, which can no longer be reconciled with
God, and thereby he transferred it to the deity itself.

---

[1] R. Bultmann, 'Polis und Hades in der Antigone des Sophokles', in *Theol. Aufs. K. Barth zum 50. Geburtstag* (1936), p. 80.

[2] W. Schadewaldt, 'Sophokles' Aias und Antigone', in *Neue
Wege zur Antike* 8 (1929), p. 114.

[3] These are the same νόμοι the divine origin of which is proclaimed in Soph. *Oed. Tyr.* 865 ff.

In so far as the Greeks felt this impracticability to be a problem at all, they gave it a tragic solution and did not regard it from the point of view of man being a sinner in the sight of the law.[1]

As a result of this antithesis, and as a supplement to the written law of the city-state, the ἄγραφος νόμος acquired from the fifth century a greater importance (Thuc. II.37.3; Pseud.-Aristot. *Rhet. Al*, 2, p. 1421b, 35 ff.).[2] It is conceived differently in detail: as an old traditional national νόμος of this or that city-state (Diog. *L.* 3.86), but usually as a natural or divine law, valid amongst all men (Xenoph. *Mem.* IV.4.19 f.; Demosth. *Or.* 18, 275, 23, 61.85; Plat. *Resp.* VIII.563d). Thus in a vague way it could be equated partly with the 'natural' law of the Sophists, partly with the universal law of the Stoics (Max. Tyr. 6, 7). Amongst the chief ἄγραφοι or ἱεροὶ νόμοι which repeatedly recur in the tradition, there are found beside the rules of religious ritual the precepts of social ethics which are already grouped together in Xenoph. *Mem.* IV.4, 20 under the designation θεοῦ νόμος. The fullest list is given in Plut. *Lib. Educ.* 10 (II.7e) (cf. Aesch. *Eum.* 545 ff.; Eur. fr. 853; Ditt Syll³ 1268). It is in line with the high regard enjoyed throughout the ages by the ἄγραφοι νόμοι that they are called by Plato the *bonds in every constitution* (Plat. *Leg.* VII.793b), and were later even regarded as the original source of all earthly laws (Archytas in Stob. *Ecl.* IV.1.132 (p. 79 Hense)).

(*d*) In the fifth century the authority of the νόμος was severely shaken, at first by the discovery of different kinds of νόμοι in the world. It is true that Herodotus still describes them with a certain respect and admiration (3.38). For he recognises in the laws of

---

[1] cf. G. Kittel, *Die Religionsgeschichte und das Urchristentum* (1932), pp. 118 ff.

[2] cf. R. Hirzel, *ΑΓΡΑΦΟΣ ΝΟΜΟΣ*, pp. 29 ff.

the nations their *wisdom* (σοφίη), and at the same time
the break-up of an original σοφίη (Hdt. 1.196 f., 7.102;
cf. Heracl. fr. 114). But soon in the ruthless struggle
for existence the subject began to make himself the
criterion of absolute validity (cf. Eur. fr. 433; Plat.
Ep. VIIII.354c). 'Human nature gained the ascendancy over the laws and became stronger than justice'
says Thucydides of the Peloponesian War (III.84,
cf. III.45.7). In Sophism the νόμος is then pushed
aside in theory too and man now sees himself only
confronted with φύσις (cf. Eur. fr. 920). A gulf is
opened up between what is just according to the law
(νόμῳ) and according to nature (φύσει) (Plat. *Gorg.*
483 ff., *Leg.* X. 889e). For the regulations of the law
are merely arbitrary, brought about by the agreement
of men (Antiphon fr. 44, col. 1.23 ff. (II.346 f. Diels[5])).
On the other hand nature has its own law which is
now the only one still to be recognised (in ethics and
politics too) as the true standard, namely the νόμος τῆς
φύσεως (Callicles in Plat. *Gorg.* 483e). Thus νόμος
remains firmly anchored to something higher. Only
this is no longer a divine being in whom one believes,
but that which has been put in its place: the φύσις
(cf. Hippocr. *Vict.* i.11).

A conception of nature, deprived of the divine
element, in which all fight against all and covetousness
(πλεονεξία) rules as the only law (Plat. *Gorg.* 483, cf.
Leg. IX.875b), was not only bound to undermine the
old law of the state which was directed towards community life, but also inevitably undermined religion
at the same time. For belief in the gods stands and
falls with reverence for the νόμος.

Yet are the gods strong, and their order strong, even Law;
for by this Law we know gods are (Eur. *Hec.* 799 f., cf.
Antiphon *Or.* 6.4). This means that if the gods refuse
to obey the law which holds sway over them (namely

that all misdeeds must be expiated [791 f.]), they have
by this act forfeited their being as gods (cf. Eur. *Ion.*
442 f.). On the other hand if they secure respect for
the just νόμος, they demonstrate the justification for
their own existence. Therefore man believes in God
and justice because of the νόμος (cf. Plat. *Menex.* 237d).
In Sophism religion is seen not only in tension with the
νόμος, but finally is unmasked as a fiction of the lawgiver (Critias fr. 25, 5 ff. [II.386 f. Diels⁵]). The νόμοι
are the clumsy handiwork of men and would not be
kept if there were no witnesses. Therefore some clever
fellow invented the punishing gods as permanent over-
seers and guarantors, particularly for secret offences.[1]
Thus according this view there are really no gods at
all; it is only the νόμος which enjoins belief in them
(cf. Plat. *Leg.* X.889e-890a).

Two things follow from this: (i) In the last resort
the νόμος can only be overthrown by an attack on
religion; such is the extent to which both are involved
with each other by their nature and their origin.
(ii) The crisis of νόμος arises from and culminates in
the world's abolishing the gods, a process which the
fifth century as it comes to an end brings with it: *this
overthrow of religion substituted the name of Nature (for God)*
(Lact. *Inst.* III.28.3). This is how Plato described it.
For him the repudiation of the sovereignty of the laws
is equivalent to apostasy from God (Plat. *Leg.* IV.701b/c
Ep. VII.336b; in the myth of the inhabitants of Atlantis
it is said: *as long as the inherited nature of the god remained
strong in them, they were submissive to the laws and kindly
disposed to their divine kindred* [*Critias* 120e]). For he
maintains that the law expresses by its actual nature

---

[1] To deal with secret sinning (cf. fr. 181 [II.181.11 ff. Diels⁵])
Democritus demands that the νόμος should stand in front of a
man's soul, i.e. that his own inner disposition should itself be
determinative for his actions (cf. fr. 264 [II.199.6 ff. Diels⁵]).

(cf. Plat. *Leg.* XII.966c) the manner of the gods' existence and activity (*Leg.* X.885b, cf. *Resp.* II.365e, *Leg.* X.904a). The νόμος determines how they are to be worshipped and conceived (Plat. *Leg.* X.890a/b). This Platonic association of 'theology' and legality is simply the philosophical expression of that which was conveyed to the early Greek world by the fact of νομίζειν θεούς (cf. p. 1).

Plato therefore undertakes to preserve the νόμος firstly by proving the existence of the gods, secondly by asserting that the νόμος being an offspring of νοῦς is related to the soul and for that reason is 'of nature' (φύσει)[1] like the latter (*Leg.* 982a ff., cf. also *Leg.* X.890d, 891b. Jambl. *Vit. Pyth.* 171, 223). By setting up the νόμος finally as divine[2] (*Ep.* VIII.354e), he defeated the Sophists' criticism of the νόμος at its crucial point.

(*e*) Socrates, in contrast to the Sophists, starts in all his thought from the νόμος as that which is the most vital constituent of the city-state. The νόμος τῆς πόλεως is so much the rule of his life that not only does he not

[1] In this connexion Plato develops the concept, aimed at Sophism, of a *proper nature* (ἔμφρων φύσις) (to use the words of a parallel passage in *Timaeus* 46d) which he here almost merges in his concept of ψυχή (*Leg.* X.891c ff.). On Plato's attitude to the law cf. A. Capelle, *Platos Dialog Politikos* (Diss., Hamburg, 1939), pp. 53 ff.

[2] *Men of sound sense have Law for their god, but men without sense Pleasure.* Here νόμος and ἡδονή are thought of on the plane of the divine as the two opposing powers. Plato, like Thucydides (II.53, III.82.8), has again and again indicated ἡδονή as the basis on which the decline of the νόμος is to be understood (*Leg.* IV.714a; *Resp.* VIII.548b, IV.429c). Life in accordance with the law is the most complete contrast to ἡδέως ζῆν (*Leg.* II.662c/663a f.). The art of the Muses, which was too much under the influence of ἡδονή, gave rise to the general lawlessness in the Athenian state (*Leg.* III.700/701a). The final result is that the νόμος βασιλεύς is succeeded by the rule of ἡδονή and λύπη (grief. *Resp.* X.607a).

act contrary to the laws, but he will go so far as to die
at their command when they are manipulated un-
justly by men. (cf. Xenoph. *Mem.* IV.4.4). Plato has
expressed this conviction of Socrates in noble fashion
in the *Crito*, when he describes the appearance of the
time-honoured Athenian Νόμοι καὶ τὸ κοινὸν τῆς πόλεως
as a kind of epiphany to Socrates in prison. A dialogue
ensues concerning the right of the individual to re-
pudiate the νόμος (*Crito* 50a ff.). In this the νόμοι
come forward as parents, providers and educators
(51c). Man is their *offspring* and *servant* (50e) and
stands in a relationship of dependence on them quite
different from that which he has on his physical
parents. These νόμοι have 'brothers in Hades' (54c),
i.e. they are valid also in the face of death and beyond.

(*f*) The relationship of Socrates to the laws of the
state provides a conspicuous example of the significance
of the νόμος for Greek ethics. Socrates does not draw
a distinction between his clear conscience and the
debased morality of the state. For the classical world
of Greece has no knowledge of a personal moral
conscience (συνείδησις),[1] but is well aware objectively
of what is right and wrong.[2] This knowledge acquires
a form in the law. Obedience to the law is righteousness (cf. Aristot. *Eth. Nicom.* 5.1, p. 1129a, 33 ff., cf.
Xenoph. *Mem.* IV.4.13 ff.). Now righteousness includes every virtue.[3] It is impossible to account in
detail for the whole of the content of the νόμος which
embraces the whole of life (cf. Aristot. *Pol.* 3.15, p.

---

[1] cf. C. A. Pierce, *Conscience in the NT* (1955).

[2] 'Conscience has no rights in the state, legality alone has them.
If conscience is to be of the right mind, it is necessary that what it
regards as right should be objective . . . and should not merely
dwell within . . .' (Hegel, *Werke* (ed. Lasson), XIII.2 (1927),
p. 127 [*Vorlesungen über die Philosophie der Religion*]), ET *Lectures on
the Philosophy of Religion*, II (1895), p. 233).

[3] cf. *Righteousness* in this series (1951), esp. pp. 9 ff.

1286a, 9 ff.), unless it is described in more general terms as in Aristot. *Eth. Nicom.* 5.4, p. 1130a, 18 ff.

The aim of all education is therefore education in the spirit and ethos of the laws (Plat. *Leg.* II.659d, cf. *Leg.* VI.751c, *Prot.* 326c/d). Indeed, the law is itself an educator, even though in a completely different sense from that of Paul in Gal. iii.24. (Plat. *Leg.* VII.809a, cf. Aristot. *Pol.* 3.16, p. 1287b, 25 f.; Archytas Pyth. in Stob. *Ecl.* IV.1.135 [p. 82, 16 f. Hense]).

Obedience to the law goes so far that it is possible to speak of *serving* (δουλεύειν) *the laws* (Plat. *Leg.* 698c, 700a, IV.715d; cf. Paul in Rom. vii.25) without any trace of the idea of disparagement which is usually connected with the term. This almost paradoxical usage enables us to realise that the νόμος exercises authority.[1] The law 'rules' (Aristot. *Pol.* 4.4 p. 1292a, 32, cf. Plat. *Leg.* IV.715d), even, according to circumstances, as δεσπότης, τύραννος (Plat. *Prot.* 337d) or βασιλεύς (Alcidamas in Aristot. *Rhet.* 3.3 p. 1406a, 23, cf. Anonym. Jambl. 6.1 [II.402.29 Diels⁵]; Plat. *Epis.* VIII.354c). He who lives according to the law, as Aristotle says (*Eth. Nicom.* x, ix.11, p. 1180a, 17 ff.), lives *by a certain intelligence and by a right system, invested with adequate sanctions*, i.e. according to an order determined by the mind which at the same time has authority to impose itself. The νόμος has coercive power (*ib.* a 21, cf. Antiphon *Or.* 6.4) which far exceeds that of an individual man (as that of a father), unless he be a βασιλεύς or similar personage. His 'servitude' to the law makes the man in the city-state (as later in the cosmos) a citizen and gives him his freedom: *it makes servants of us all only to set us free* (Cic. *Pro Cluent.* 53.146;

[1] It is said that Pittacus answered the question of king Croesus concerning the greatest authority by pointing to the νόμοι (Diod. S. *Excerpta Vaticana* 7.27; Diog. *L.* 1.77).

cf. Plat. *Leg*. III.701b; Aristot. *Pol*. 5.9, p. 1310a 34 ff.), distinguishing him from the slave who by his very nature has no part in the νόμοι (TGF fr. adesp. 326).

Apart from the νόμοι, there is no question of a servitude (δουλεία) in the positive sense except with regard to the gods (especially Apollo of Delphi) (cf. Soph. *Oed. Tyr*. 410; Eur. *Orest*. 418, *Ion*, 309; Plat. *Phaedr*. 85b). For to be subject to the laws means at the same time to serve the gods (Plat. *Leg*. VI.762e, cf. Plat. *Ep*. VIII.354e). The νόμιμος is not only the δίκαιος,[1] but also the εὐσεβής (Xenoph. *Mem*. IV.6.2). This seems to be the Delphic view of religion in particular, to which Socrates also adhered (Xenophon *Mem*. I.3.1, cf. IV.3.16). Amongst the various traditional instructions attributed to Apollo of Delphi, the saying is found[2]: *Follow God: obey the law* (Stob. *Ecl*. III.1.173 [125.5 Hense]). Following God and obeying the law are placed side by side without any interrelationship.[3]

For the sovereignty of the law, together with the blessing of the gods, guarantees the stability of the state and the possibility of existence for man (Plat. *Leg*. IV.715d). This 'soteriological function remained a permanent characteristic of the νόμος (cf. Pseud.-Plat. *Min*. 314d; Aristot. *Rhet*. 1.4, p. 1360a 19 f.; Dio Chrys. *Or*. 58.1 [Budé]; Porphyr. *Marc*. 25; Letter of Aristeas 240; Just. *Apol*. 1.65.1). But it is only when it is obeyed from conviction that *it shows* to them *their own particular virtue* (Democr. fr. 248 [II.194.18 ff. Diels⁵]). Without the νόμος mankind would have to lead a life of the beasts (Plut. *Col*. 30.1 [II.1124d] from Plat. *Leg*. IX.874e).

(*g*) Plato interprets the death of Socrates, obediently

---

[1] cf. *Righteousness* in this series, p. 13.

[2] cf. W. H. Roscher, *Philol*., 59 (1900), pp. 37 f.

[3] M. Ant. (7.31) took up the saying of Apollo about following God by way of the law, but gave it a Stoic interpretation.

defying the law, as the transition of that which was the norm and the law from the institutions of the state to the ψυχή of Socrates, i.e. to the mind.

Within the human ψυχή, as it was disclosed to the Greeks by the example of Socrates, Plato seeks and finds a κόσμος and a τάξις (using a medical analogy). Medicine clearly possessed for the normal condition of the body no single name, but spoke of health, strength, beauty and the like. But for the κόσμος and the τάξις of the soul Plato used one word only: νόμος (cf. Plat Gorg. 504c, Crito 53c, Phileb. 26d).

Here we have the foundation of the 'state' and the ideal legislation of the 'Νόμοι' by Plato (cf. Leg. XII.960d). Its new, inner νόμος is that of which the τάξις is determined by the standard of the ψυχή, i.e. δικαιοσύνη and σωφροσύνη.[1] In Plato this law is 'begotten'[2] anew out of a generally valid principle, knowledge (Plat. Leg. X.890d; cf. I.645a/b; IV.712a). That which manifests itself through the νόμοι is the mind. In an etymological play upon words, which always reveals a real relationship of ideas, Plato calls the νόμος the reason's ordering (τοῦ νοῦ διανομή) Leg.

[1] The opposite of this is found in Plat. Leg. V.728a/b: violation and neglect of the laws make the soul bad.

[2] cf. Plat. Symp. 209d: Solon is highly esteemed among you for begetting his laws. The use of this metaphor places Plato in a venerable tradition. Sophocles lets the eternal νόμοι likewise be 'engendered' (Oed. Tyr. 865 ff.) and 'live' (Ant. 457); their begetter is Olympus and no dead human native has 'brought them forth' (Oed. Tyr. 869 ff.). The laws which Lycurgus left are called in Plat. Symp. 209c 'children' and the νόμοι which appear to Socrates in prison refer to their 'brothers' in Hades' (Plat. Crito 54c). The growing up of the νόμοι in Heraclitus (cf. fr. 114 (176.7 f. Diels[5])) also belongs in this biological realm of ideas. The continuing influence of the Platonic formulation is seen in Josephus (Ant. 4.319) who otherwise knows nothing of a begetting (cf. TWNT, I, p. 667) by God, but says of the Jewish laws: laws which he (i.e. God), the begetter of them, presented to you himself.

IV.714a; cf. XII.967c II.674b). According to Aristotle the dominion of the νοῦς is embodied in the coercive power of the νόμος (*Eth. Nic.* 10, p. 1180a 21). To make νόμος rule in the state is to make God and the reason alone to be the sovereign (Aristot. *Pol.* III.xi.4, p. 1287a 28 ff.). By being firmly anchored to the νοῦς the Greek concept of law once more acquires in a philosophic form an absolute validity. For it is thereby tied afresh to the divine (Plat. *Leg.* IV.713a/c).

Contrasted with this it is a revolutionary idea, pointing towards the future of Hellenism, when the same Plato advances for the first time the thesis that the ideal is not the rule of the law, which necessarily always lags behind progress, but the rule of the just and royal person who possesses true knowledge (*Pol.* 294a/b; cf. Plat. *Leg.* IX.875c/d). In Aristotle too (*Pol.* 3.13, p. 1284a 3 ff.) there appears the man who towers above all others by his excellence (ἀρετή), no longer bound by any law. He does not only stand above the νόμος, but he is, as a god among men (10 f.), himself the law for himself and for others (13 f.; cf. *Eth. Nic.* 14, p. 1128a 32; Plut. *Alex.* 52 (I.694 f.)).

3. νόμος in Hellenism

(a) In Hellenism this philosophical theory became historical reality. The νόμος no longer rules in the city-state as 'king', but the will and the person of the βασιλεύς has itself become νόμος (Dio Chrys. *Or.* 3.43 [Budé]; cf. Anaxarch. in Plut. *Alex.* 52.I.694 f.). The god-king is the new divine source of the νόμος which is connected with him in a special manner (Themist. *Or.* 9, p. 123a (Dindorf); cf. Isoc. *Demonax* 36; Isis hymn from Andros 4 f. (p. 15 Peek)) and is in part expressly called after him βασιλικὸς νόμος (Pseud.-Plat. *Min.* 317a/c; Ditt. *Or* II.483.1 [Pergamon]; cf. I.329.14

James ii.8).[1] Corresponding to his worship as living
image (Ditt. *Or.* 90.3) and imitator of Zeus (Muson.
p. 37, 3 ff. [Hense]) the king, or alternatively the
philosopher, is himself even considered to be the visible
manifestation of the eternal law in the cosmos, as a
νόμος ἔμψυχος (Muson. p. 37, 2 ff.; Archytas Pyth. in
Stob. *Ecl.* IV.1.135 [p. 82, 20 f. Hense]; Diotogenes
Pyth. in Stob. *Ecl.* IV.7.61 [p. 263, 19 Hense]; Philo
Vit. Mos. 2.4).[2]

(*b*) In Stoicism, where the 'law' is a fundamental
concept, the place of the πολιτικὸς νόμος of the classical
period which had grown up historically, is taken by a
cosmic and universal νόμος. The designation νόμος in
its proper sense is no longer appropriate to the laws of
the state[3]; they have sunk to be false ideas (δόξαι
ψευδεῖς) [Max. Tyr. 6.5 (Hobein)]. The individual
in Hellenism now seeks and finds the only true and
divine νόμος in the cosmos alone (cf. Plut. *De Exilio* 5
[II.601b]). The world is his 'state'. Here a homogeneous law holds sway (Chrysipp. fr. 323 [III.79.38 ff.
von Arnim]; Plut. *Alex. Fort. Virt.* 1.6 [II.329a];
Philo *Op. Mund.* 143), and this, as the foundation of all
communal life, also unites men and gods (Chrysipp.
fr. 335 [III.82.18 von Arnim]). Since it is the universal
supreme reason (M. Ant. 7.9), this νόμος pervades the
whole of nature just as it determines the moral conduct
of men (Chrysipp. fr. 314 [III.77.34 ff. von Arnim]).
The world order, as determined by the mind, is identical
with the concept of law. This in its turn is founded in
the last resort on the religious sense, whether the νόμος

[1] cf. Eus. *De Laude Constantini* (p. 201, 27) of Constantine.

[2] cf. E. R. Goodenough, 'The Political Philosophy of Hellenic
Kingship', in *Yale Class. Studies*, 1 (1928), pp. 55 ff.

[3] The νόμος of the city-state is used only for purposes of comparison: God is for the world what the law is in the state, as is
explained by Pseud.-Aristot. *Mund.* 6, p. 400b 7 ff. (cf. Epictet.
Diss. I.12.7 *et passim*).

is set up directly as a θεός (II.315.23 v. Arnim) or the deity is identified with the law of the cosmos, itself unmoved[1] yet moving all things (Pseud.-Aristot. *Mund.* 6, p. 400b 28 ff.). This is accommodated with popular religion by giving the world-νόμος the name of Zeus (Zeno fr. 162 [I.43 von Arnim=Diog. *L.* 7.88]). In the hymns of Cleanthes too (fr. 537 [I.121 ff. von Arnim]), it is the almighty Zeus who on the one hand guides the universe by means of the νόμος (v.2), and on the other is placed in the final verses on an equality with the world-order itself, and the right to glorify this is the highest honour for men and gods (v. 38 f. [I.123.4 f. von Arnim]).[2]

Thus man must make a decision, by virtue of the νοῦς or λόγος which dwells within him, for the νόμος and a life in conformity with it (Plut. *Stoic. Rep.* 1 [II.1033b]). But in doing so he does not obey an absolute demand approaching from without or from another world, but he comes to himself and gains his freedom (Chrysipp. fr. 360 [III.87.43 f. von Arnim], cf. Max. Tyr. 33.5; M. Ant. 10.25). Therefore it is not fundamentally impossible to fulfil the law; on the contrary it is that to which the striving and destiny of man is directed by nature. Thus the *law of nature and of God* or the *divine law*, which Epictetus proclaims (*Diss.* I.29.13/19) is as regards its content simply the moral law of philosophy[3] (cf. *Diss.* II.16.28, cf. I.29.4). For Epictetus it is the laws which issue thence (*Diss.* IV.3.11/12), which alone lead to the life of bliss. When the philosopher follows them of his own accord,

[1] For the immutability of the law cf. Plat. *Leg.* XII.960d; Pseud.-Plat. *Min.* 321b; Max. Tyr. 11.12; Plut. *Vit. Lycurg.* 29 (I.57d); Philo *Op. Mund.* 61. Cf. M. Mühl, pp. 88 ff.

[2] cf. also Heracl. fr. 114 (v. 24 f. [I.122, 20 f. von Arnim]).

[3] cf. A. Bonhoeffer, 'Epiktet und das NT', in RVV 10 (1911), pp. 154 f.

he is free and a friend of God (*Diss*. IV.3.9). For in doing so, he follows God.[1] This is made clear if we combine the sayings of Plutarch in *Ad Principem Ineruditum* 3.1(II.780c) and in *Aud*. 1 (II.37d).

Thus whilst on the one hand the νόμος has undergone an expansion into the cosmic order, on the other hand it has been given a markedly inward quality. It is now, as it were, written within the man, on his soul (Max. Tyr. 6),[2] so that M. Ant. X.13.2 names it beside πίστις, αἰδώς, ἀλήθεια and ἀγαθὸς δαίμων amongst the most valuable elements in human nature.

(c) Neo-Platonism added no more new features to the Greek concept of law. Other basic motifs had replaced in it the fundamental Platonic and Stoic ideas about the law. In Plotinus the νόμος plays only a subordinate role in ethics and the doctrine of the soul. A life of bliss cannot be bestowed on those who have not done what makes them worthy of bliss (Plot. *Enn*. III.2.4 towards the end). This is the will of οἱ ἐν τῷ παντὶ νόμοι (*Enn*. III.2.8). Plotinus recognises in this the operation of the divine will which by the νόμος of providence maintains man in existence (Plot. *Enn*. III.2.9). The Gnostic teaching is reproached with disparaging together with divine foreknowledge also 'all the lawfulness of the world' and bringing ἀρετή into ridicule (*Enn*. II.9.15). For all wrongdoing is punished and nothing can escape that which is settled ἐν τῷ τοῦ παντὸς νόμῳ (*Enn*. III.2.4). This applies also in the case of the various reincarnations of the soul.[3] The Neo-Platonist Porphyry then developed in addition

---

[1] In Muson. (p. 86, 19 ff. Hense) the ideal life for a Stoic sage appears as the law of Zeus.

[2] cf. Jul. *Or*. 7, p. 209c (cf. Paul in Rom. ii.15); cf. Plot. *Enn*. V.3.4; Procl. in *Rem. Publ*. II.307.7 ff. (Kroll).

[3] With reference to Plat. *Phaedr*. 248c, *Tim*. 41e; in the Hermetic literature cf. Stob. *Ecl*. I.49.49 (=p. 418, 6 Hense), I.49.69 (=p. 463, 23 Hense).

a detailed doctrine in three stages concerning the νόμος (*Ad Marc.* 25/27).

(*d*) The later ancient world goes back in the main to the 'Orphic' and Platonic conceptions of νόμος (especially Plat. *Leg.* IV.716a = *Orph. Fr.* 21 [Kern]; *Gorg.* 523a; *Phaedr.* 248c; *Tim.* 41e *et passim*), but gives them a cosmic theological interpretation (Procl. in *Rem. Publ.* II.307.20 ff. [Kroll], cf. in *Tim.* I.203.28 f.). Beside the one world-creating νόμος which ranks as god and associate of Zeus (*Orph. Fr.* 160 [Kern], cf. Procl. in *Tim.* I.156.9 ff., cf. *Orph. Fr.* 159 [Kern]) there is an elaborately organised system of cosmic νόμοι (Procl. in *Tim.* I.136.13 ff., 397.22 ff.) which are given a comprehensive unity in Adrasteia (Nemesis, cf. Hermias in Plat. *Phaedr.* 248c [p. 161, 15 ff. Couvr] = *Orph. Fr.* 105 [Kern]).

4. *The Greek concept of νόμος and the New Testament*

In contrast to every law derived from revelation, νόμος for the Greeks originated in the mind (νοῦς). So the genuine νόμος is no mere obligatory law, but something in which an entity valid in itself is discovered and appropriated (Pseud.-Plat. *Min.* 315a, cf. Plat. *Polit.* 300c/e). It is 'the order which exists (from time immemorial), is valid and is put into operation. It does not simply set in order, but orders, does not simply command, demand and forbid, but rules. This order as it were brings its own fulfilment and in the event of non-fulfilment imposes its will or is upheld'.[1] This aspect of the nature of the νόμος has something in common with the Greek gods.[2] This is the only ex-

---

[1] cf. H. Cremer, *Biblisch-theologisches Wörterbuch des nt.lichen Griechisch*, rev. by J. Kögel ([11]1923), p. 749. Cf. Xenoph. *Mem.* IV.4.24; Plat. *Leg.* IV.716a; Plot. *Enn.* IV.3.13/24.

[2] This is often stated by way of comparison, e.g. by Aristot. *Pol.* e.13, p. 1284a 10; Pseud.-Aristot. *Mund.* 6. p. 400b 7 ff.

c

planation of the command: *we must keep to the laws of
our country just as though they were some gods of second rank*
(Hierocles Stoicus in Stob. *Ecl.* III.39.36 [p. 733, 10 f.]).
The νόμος, like the gods, has a supreme and terrible
power over all those who wish to evade it. At the same
time it is like them surrounded by a supremely ideal
quality because it is the only σωτηρία (cf. p. 15) for all
who obey it (Eur. *Ba.* 890 ff.). It is a simple logical
consequence that the νόμος of the city-state as well as
that of the cosmos, now appears in fact again and again
also as 'god' (TGF fr. adesp. 471, cf. Plat. *Ep.* 8.354e;
Pind. fr. 169; Aristot. *Pol.* 3.16, p. 1287a 28 ff.; Procl. in
Rem. Publ. II.307.20 [Kroll]; Philodem. Philos. *Pietat.*11
[II.315.23 von Arnim]), called in mythological theology
Zeus (Plut. *Ad Principem Ineruditum* 4.2 [II.781b], cf.Zeno
fr. 162 ([I.43 von Arnim = Diog. *L.* 7.88]; cf. p. 3 f.).

By understanding the concept of law in this way the
Greek world, from the point of view of the NT, con-
cealed from itself the true meaning of the law. For a
Greek never thought of the law as something which, when
correctly understood, would destroy him or make him
despair of himself, because it makes a man conscious of
the fact that he cannot keep it.[1] On the contrary the
later ancient world was in the end brought to despair[2]
because it no longer possessed an objective historical
νόμος and even philosophy could no longer give it one.

[1] No Greek could speak, as Paul does in Rom. ii.23, of νόμος
τῆς ἁμαρτίας (cf. I Cor. xv.56). For to Greek eyes the law cannot
be at the same time a cause of transgressing the law (Chrysipp.
fr. 1125 [II.326.35 v. Arnim]).

[2] cf. the pious wish of Celsus in Orig. *Cels.* 8.72: *Would that it
were possible to unite under one law the inhabitants of Asia, Europe and
Libya, both Greeks and barbarians even at the furthest limits* (cf. H.
Chadwick, *Origen: Contra Celsum* (1953), p. 507, n. 1). The νόμος
Christi (cf. Just. *Dial.* 11) has taken the place of the individual
national νόμοι of the ancient world as well as of much of the Stoic
ideal of the homogeneous and all-embracing νόμος. Cf. E.
Peterson, *Der Monotheismus als politisches Problem* (1935), pp. 62 f.

II. LAW IN THE OLD TESTAMENT

1. *Early Israelite law*

LITERARY and form criticism have made it possible to pick out from amongst the whole stock of the OT legal literature the earliest corpora of Israelite law so as to reveal the fundamental features of early Israelite law.[1] Particular examples of these old legal corpora are the groups of five-unit sayings,[2] probably originally twelve in number, in each case with the ending *shall surely be put to death*[3]; in addition, the groups of four-unit sayings, also twelve originally, beginning with *cursed*[4] and the so-called Decalogue which was historically the most influential.[5] This last has indeed abandoned complete symmetry of form for the sake of its contents, but on the other hand it enables the essentials of those ancient laws to be perceived all the more distinctly.

The situation in life of these Israelite laws was that act which was performed regularly at the central shrine[6] to renew and commemorate Yahweh's covenant

---

[1] For the following see especially Alt, *Die Ursprünge des israelitischen Rechts*, pp. 33 ff.

[2] i.e. sayings consisting of a poetic line with five 'stresses'.

[3] Exod. xxi.12, 15-17, xxii.18 f., xxxi.14 f.; Lev. xx.2, 9-16, 27, xxiv.16, xxvii.29. The original precepts can be recovered in part only by reconstruction, cf. Alt pp. 45 f.

[4] Deut. xxvii.15-26 with small emendations.

[5] Exod. xx.2 ff.; Deut. v.6 ff. On the question of the original form of the decalogue cf. L. Köhler, 'Der Dekalog', ThR (1929), pp. 161 ff.

[6] cf. M. Noth, *Das System der 12 Stämme Israels* (1930), (cf. *History of Israel* (ET ²1960), pp. 100 ff. Possibly the essential cult-object was the ark of Yahweh in which were perhaps preserved simply the laws of the covenant. Cf. P. Volz, *Mose und sein Werk*

with Israel. For the origin of these laws we must look
to Sinai and to a special event there, the details of
which will certainly be difficult to elucidate.[1]

These statements about the presumed situation in
life of these laws in the period of the judges must
correspond to and be interpreted by what they themselves reveal about their theological situation in Israel's
belief in God. Now this 'situation' of the law is the
conception of the covenant.[2] Yahweh has chosen Israel
to be his people, Israel has acknowledged this Yahweh
to be its God. This basic proposition of the whole
OT[3] is the immediate foundation of these laws. They
are an expression of Yahweh's claim to reign over the
whole life of the people belonging to him in virtue of
his choice. This is declared as clearly as possible by
the first commandment of the Decalogue.

Thus these laws are not understood as an equitable
adjustment of men's vital interests, perhaps with
divine sanction. Nor when they are obeyed is this an
achievement which Israel of its own accord offers to its
God in thanks for covenant and election. It is certainly
not an achievement by means of which the people
would come to belong to the deity. These laws are in
the strict sense demands made by the God to whom
this people belongs because he has revealed himself to

([2]1932), pp. 100 ff.; Galling in RGG[2] III, cols. 1449 f. Cf. the
discussion by M. Haran in IEJ 9 (1959), pp. 30 ff., 89 ff.

[1] Although it seems that it was the priests who recited the law
(Deut. xxxi.11, xxxiii.10), tradition points to Moses, who was not
a priest, for the Decalogue. There is no decisive reason against
this tradition. Cf. Volz, pp. 20 ff.; Köhler, pp. 178 ff., 18.4

[2] W. Eichrodt, *Theologie des AT*, I ([2]1939), pp. 26 ff., ET
Theology of the OT (1961), pp. 70 ff.; Volz, pp. 73 f. It must
be admitted that the conception of election was not yet present in
its later theological form. [Cf. also H. H. Rowley, *The Biblical
Doctrine of Election* (1950).]

[3] Contrary to e.g. L. Köhler, *Theologie des AT* (1936), p. 12
(ET 1953), p. 30.

it by bringing it out of Egypt and because he has shown himself in every way, both up till then and for the future, to be its God. So the motive for keeping this law is simply obedience, although in fact it is hardly possible to detect that conscious thought has been given to the motive for fulfilling the law.

Now the nature of the law in detail is in line with all this:

(a) *Its demand is absolute.* This is shown in the style of these series of laws, in their forcefulness, in their uncompromising wording, which estimates the deed as such and gives no place to hidden difficulties or particular circumstances. Moreover this can be seen in the punishment threatened which can only be death, that is, being rooted out from the people of God, or cursing, which hands the wrongdoer over to God's destructive power, when the deed concerned is beyond the reach of men. It is even more evident in the fact that this law can also be formulated without the mention of any punishment for its transgression; it appears not even in the imperative or jussive form, elsewhere usual, but simply as the indicative: *Thou shalt not kill.*[1]

(b) *The negative character of these commands or, consequently rather, of these prohibitions.* In this way again it is distinctly confirmed that the theological situation of this law is the covenant of election. It is not a matter of commanding that which makes a man belong to God, but of forbidding that which abolishes this relationship.

(c) *But the laws are not thereby prevented from displaying an element of encouragement to obey.* This is shown in the manner by which it is intended to impress the proclamation of the law on the will of the hearer and to make its infringement impossible from within the man by the reminder of Yahweh's deeds. But the encouragement consists by no means in the promise

[1] For this whole subject cf. Alt pp. 37 ff.; Volz p. 26.

of a reward simply because the covenant precedes the prohibition. The 'reward' can thus consist only in remaining in this positive relationship to Yahweh.[1] In consequence mention is made of the judgement for transgression, but not of a special reward for observing the law.

(*d*) *Furthermore in spite of its brevity this law is comprehensive*. It is not only the cult of Yahweh, but the whole of life which stands under the law. The claim of this God to rule leaves no neutral zone. And yet it is not in the nature of these laws to deal in detailed casuistry, however much in the course of time more precise catalogues became necessary, to a certain extent as regulations for carrying out particular instances of these basic prohibitions.[2]

(*e*) *Finally it is in the nature of these laws that they are addressed to Israel as a whole*. The individual is treated as a member of the nation, and the neighbour whom the law indicates is the member of the nation. Thus the punishment too in the event of the law being violated is the affair of the whole body. Hence the method of inflicting death is stoning, in which all take part (Deut. xiii.9 f.),[3] and in the case of a murder which has not been cleared up the nearest community is under the obligation to make atonement (Deut. xxi.1 ff.).

With this the object of the law has already been described. The intention is to guarantee that the nation and the individual are bound to Yahweh alone. Hence *thou shalt have no other gods beside me*. Hence the dissociation from all magic and sorcery.[4] The rest is

---

[1] e.g. the promise (admittedly perhaps secondary) in the commandment concerning honouring parents.

[2] Detailed evidence in Alt pp. 49 ff.

[3] [For another interpretation of stoning, cf. Köhler, *Hebrew Man* (1956), p. 112.]   [4] cf. Volz pp. 27 ff., 40 ff.

connected with this: the shaping of the nation as the people of God, the exclusion of those actions which disturb the dealings of the members one with another and endanger the life of the whole community. But at the same time it must be kept firmly in mind that the validity of the law is not based on its suitability for social purposes, but on the will of the God of the covenant who stands behind it. Thus the object of the law is to settle the relationship of the covenant-nation and of the individual to the God of the covenant and to the members of the nation who belong to the same God. Because this nation has been chosen by this God this is to be done by excluding those things which invalidate or disturb the relationship.[1]

2. *The understanding of law in the earlier historical books*

The understanding of law which we find expressed in the early Israelite corpora is in line with the interpretation of Israel's history given by the 'Yahwist' and 'Elohist' sources, particularly with regard to the position assigned to the law. Even though J and E are not brought to an end until the promise that Palestine will be conquered by Israel has been fulfilled,[2] yet in both of them the period when the law was given is the culmination. The preparation for it is made by presenting the history up till then from the point of view of the wholly undeserved election of Israel from among the nations. So it is made abundantly clear how little this election depends on the part played by the nation.[3] It is just this story of the merciful dealings of God with

---

[1] cf. the awakening of the consciousness of being Israel (Judges xix f.); Noth pp. 100 ff., Volz p. 500.

[2] cf. H. Holzinger, *Einleitung in den Hexateuch* (1893), pp. 71 ff.

[3] Neither naturally (since Ishmael and Esau were the first-born) nor morally (cf. the story of Jacob, the journey through the wilderness).

the often rebellious people which reaches its climax in the fact that Yahweh reveals himself to the whole nation, makes himself to be its God, the nation to be his people (Exod. xix). This event gives to the law its meaning as the divine gift intended to show the people what conduct is appropriate to its position as a people in God's possession, and alternatively what undermines this position. Thus the law is a demonstration of his mercy by showing how the people lives in the sight of God, because it lives through Him. Since 'God the deliverer gives the law' in this way, 'obedience has been made the proof of faith'.[1]

As regards its contents, the law accepted in these historical books, in addition to the early Israelite corpora, consists principally of the Book of the Covenant.[2] This contains in addition to early Israelite matter the law practised by the pre-Israelite inhabitants of Palestine. Its chief tendency is to take over and permeate with the religion of Yahweh the pre-Israelite law which had been adopted.[3] It is an essential point here that no conscious distinction is yet made between law and morality.[4] Again, these precepts acquire their validity only owing to the fact that they are established by God, not because of their inherent goodness or usefulness. It is true that God demands

[1] A. Schlatter, *Einleitung in die Bibel* ([4]1923), p. 15.

[2] The Book of the Covenant (Exod. xxi-xxiii) probably dates from the Palestinian period before the monarchy, but was no doubt for a long time after that still the basis of the law. Cf. Procksch pp. 231 f.; A. Jepsen, *Untersuchungen zum Bundesbuch* (1927), pp. 96 ff.; Alt pp. 18, 25 ff.

[3] Eichrodt I, pp. 28 ff. (ET pp. 75 ff.); Jepsen pp. 100 ff.

[4] To consider this, as e.g. Jepsen pp. 102 ff. does, to be a misfortune, is to take a modern view. Whether this judgement corresponds to the facts is open to question. The principle of placing law and morality side by side is derived from the whole OT conception of God.

the good, but it is to be performed because God demands it.

Another kind of laws consists of the divine ordinances which regulate the cult. They are understood to be the ones by which Yahweh himself determines the worship to be offered to him (Exod. xx.24b).[1] This means too that no worship originated with men, nor is it offered freely as their own achievement, but that the only 'lawful' worship of God is that which is brought into being by the fact that God has revealed himself to the nation and which consists in the recognition of that fact. However fragmentary and primitive the cult-law may be of which these narrators tell us, yet this, their basic understanding of the cult, is perfectly clear, that it is the gracious directive of God telling the people how it may worship the holy God, indeed how it must do so. This involves the fact that the cult and the practice of the law cannot be separated if the law in J and E is to be understood.

Consistent with this is the early usage of priestly legislation in the narrower sense and the understanding of the law expressed in it. The main contents of the special priestly instructions for the cult is the rule concerning clean and unclean. Here the essential point is that this whole instruction concerning the question of clean and unclean is imparted by order of Yahweh and as his commandment. The question is not: what will have the most influence with the deity? but: what does Yahweh appoint as the worship due to him from his people? But the task of the priest is not only to give directions about clean and unclean. He has also to declare at the national assemblies the law as handed down, and to preserve it at the shrine. Furthermore

[1] Kautzsch, *Die heilige Schrift des AT* ([4]1922), I p. 127 f. translates: *In every place in which I cause you to honour my name.* Admittedly the meaning is not quite clear.

he is concerned with the divine judgement in those difficult cases in which the community approaches the shrine for a legal decision.[1] This does not mean that the priest actually exercises a judicial function. The relationship between priest and law makes it proper to look for the formation of the Book of the Covenant in priestly circles.[2]

All law is the will of Yahweh; the reason for this is the fact that Yahweh has made this nation his own by a historical event and now wishes to see it living as befits his property. But since the relationship of Yahweh to his people is a matter of history, there is nothing incompatible in this understanding of the law, if the law itself is seen as coming into being in the course of history. It is nevertheless to be considered the law of God, and this is expressed by connecting all valid law with the revelation of God at Sinai. This connexion is therefore not so much a historical as a theological judgement.

3. *The attitude of the prophets to the law*

The preaching of the prophets is based on a fresh meeting with God and on the reality of this God breaking into the midst of the devout life of the nation, a life which is in fact godless. The essence and basis of the prophets' preaching is not a fresh idea of God, but a fresh meeting with him.[3] This also explains the attitude of the prophets to the law. They do not suppose that they must first inform the people of what Yahweh demands. Their preaching presupposes that man has been told what is good and what the Lord expects from

[1] L. Köhler, *Die hebräische Rechtsgemeinde* (Züricher Rektoratsrede (1931)), pp. 13 ff.; ET 'Justice in the Gate' in *Hebrew Man* (1956), p. 163.   [2] Procksch p. 230; Jepsen pp. 99 f.
[3] For the following cf. Eichrodt I pp. 185 ff. (ET pp. 345 ff.); K. Marti, *Geschichte der israelitischen Religion* ([5]1907), pp. 184 ff.

him (Mic. vi.8). Certainly the prophets often put this will of God into a fresh form and add new features to it, but without being themselves conscious or making others conscious of bringing forward for the first time a hitherto unknown demand. Indeed the prophets' preaching acknowledges not only the law but also its basis: Israel is the people whom God has chosen (Amos ii.9, iii.2; Isa. i.2; Hos. viii.13 ff.). To break the law is apostasy from Yahweh (Isa. i.27 ff.). The prophets throughout condemn the infringement of the commandments (Amos v.7, 10 ff.; Hos. v.10, iv.2; Jer. vii.9). Hos. viii.12 even expressly assumes a written law.

But there is nevertheless comparatively seldom any direct appeal to the precisely formulated law, such as the Decalogue or the Book of the Covenant (Hos. iv.2; Jer. vii.9); and where it occurs no special emphasis is given to it. In view of what has been said, this can be explained neither as due to ignorance nor to rejection of what the law contains. There remain only two explanations of this situation: a definite realisation by the prophets of the nature of the law, and the different objective of the prophets' preaching.

As regards the first point: the prophets were met by the fact that it was possible for men to combine an appeal to the law and its wording with a refusal of genuine obedience and with uncharitableness towards one's neighbour[1] (Amos ii.6, viii.4 ff.; Jer. viii.8). They therefore express the law in its simplest terms, as when Amos says: *Hate evil and do good* (Amos v.15). This is not intended to represent the overriding of a narrow viewpoint in favour of a 'purely ethical' one,[2]

---

[1] cf. Eichrodt I pp. 198 f., ET p. 374; Marti pp. 184 ff.

[2] cf. Marti p. 169: The good in the universally human, international, purely ethical meaning, namely that which must be regarded at all times and everywhere as good.

but the resistance to attempts at introducing disobedience through the gaps in the fence of the official and outwardly respected law (cf. Hos. vi.6; Mic. vi.8). When the law is thus reduced to its simplest terms, it is at the same time deepened and unified, and so the real meaning of the old law, e.g. the Decalogue, is discovered. The law is not to replace complete obedience to the God who in direct and vital challenge meets his people and the individual; it is therefore not quoted and used directly, although it is recognised as an institution set up by Yahweh.

But there is the second point too: in view of the meeting with God which had been granted them and of their judgement of the people's situation as seen from this experience, the prophets could no longer expect salvation to derive from a life ordered in accordance with the law, particularly now that the will of Yahweh had been grasped in this fundamental manner. A fresh chance still exists for Israel only in the free activity of God who miraculously creates new things, for which the prophets are looking; 'It is only when there is some vision of a new existence for the nation beyond the annihilation of the present order, that the divine imperatives are brought out more strongly.'[1] After judgement and renewal, Jerusalem will be called *the city of righteousness* (Isa. i.26); even the heathen too will come to the new Zion to receive *tōrāh* (Isa. ii.3). The prophets' attitude to the law, affirming and at the same time criticising and abolishing it (this is seldom expressed, but does in fact happen) is intelligible on no other grounds than their being directly possessed by the divine holiness.

It is only with this fundamental attitude in mind that we can understand the position of the prophets with regard to the divine service in the narrower sense,

[1] Eichrodt I p. 190, ET p. 359 f.

namely the cult.[1] The cult, as the prophets find it, serves to cover up disobedience, and to gain control over God. Wrongdoing and lack of love are linked with this cult, indeed they actually find their justification in it. Consequently conflict arises between the prophets and this manner of serving God (Jer. vii.11; Hos. iv.6; Zeph. iii.4b; Jer. ii.8). Some sayings of the prophets certainly go even further and completely reject the cult[2] as not being appointed by God (Amos v.25; Isa. i.12; Jer. vii.22). It seems that they did not think that the manner of worshipping God was remediable. The essential point is that the prophets' censure does not propose a manner of worshipping God without a cult, but that this censure can be understood only by discerning the incongruity between the God who calls his people to account and the activities of the public worship as known to the prophets which ostensibly serves the honour of God.

4. How Deuteronomy understands the law

Deuteronomy contains a conception, complete in itself, of the law of Yahweh, which, in the original form of the book,[3] is consistently applied in the admission and modification of mainly old legal material. The characteristic quality of this concept of the law

[1] For the following see especially Eichrodt I 193 ff., ET pp. 364 ff.; E. K. Kautzsch, *Biblische Theologie des AT* (1911), pp. 233 ff. [Cf. also, on recent literature, H. H. Rowley 'Ritual and the Hebrew Prophets' in S. H. Hooke, *Myth, Ritual and Kingship* (1958), pp. 236-60.]

[2] cf. P. Volz, 'Die radikale Ablehnung der Kultreligion durch die alttestamentlichen Propheten', ZSTh (1937) 63 ff. [But many scholars would disagree with Volz, and would interpret the prophetic sayings differently; cf. Rowley *op. cit.* in previous note, esp. pp. 241 ff.]

[3] Especially the passages in which the first person singular (or 'I') is used in the speeches. Cf. in particular G. von Rad, *Das Gottesvolk im Dt.* (1929), for this point and on this whole section.

lies firstly in the emphasis with which the law's demand is based on the action of God, by which He had made Israel to be His people, to be a *holy people*. Deuteronomy emphasises no less strongly than JE that the religious and national existence of the Israelite people rests solely upon the covenant sworn to their forefathers (iv.32 ff.; vii.9, 12 ff.; ix.5 *et passim*). It is therefore a main task of the law to guard the exclusive bond of Israel with this God. Consequently it carries on a passionate warfare against *other gods*. No doubt the struggle for one place in which to worship the one God is connected with this (xiii.7 ff.). Secondly it is part of the peculiarity of the Deuteronomic law that a serious effort is made to enable the individual member of the nation to share in the blessing of this relationship to God. In Deuteronomy the fate of the individual too is certainly closely bound up with that of the whole people, but the emphasis now lies very heavily on the proper distribution of duties and particularly of the rights of the individual members of the people of God, so that none may lack the blessing of God in this life.

This distinctive quality of the whole book provides the clue to the characteristic features of Deuteronomy considered in detail:

(*a*) Deuteronomy in its proclamation of the law is in fact also a sermon, not a colourless enumeration of legal standards, but exhortation[1] which aims at arousing a joyous performance of the law out of gratitude for what God has done, and this is evident from the whole plan of the book. The people is to be confronted not with a legal code, but with the living God himself who will not let himself be hidden behind his law. All teaching about the law is first of all teaching

---

[1] cf. for this especially H. Breit, *Die Predigt des Deuteronomisten* (1933), p. 228 *et passim*.

about God's activity[1]; the law gives this history actuality in the present. In line with this is the trend towards greater inwardness, which shows itself for example in the phrase found several times *with all your heart and with all your soul* (vi.5; x.12; xxvi.16 *et passim*) or in the summons to cleave closely to Yahweh (x.20; xxx.20). Thus there must not only be an outward observance of the law, but all actual behaviour must be rooted in the love of God in the heart.

(*b*) This law is to embrace every sphere of life, even if it is more interested in 'ethics' than in 'ritual'.[2] Yet in spite of this comprehensive character this law does not try casuistically to regulate all the eventualities of life. Its aim is rather to point out the general lines (cf. e.g. in the legislation concerning the cult how little interest is shown in complete correctness).

(*c*) The principal objective of Deuteronomy is to show the obligation to one's neighbour, in fact to one's fellow-countryman.[3] Its motive is not humanitarianism but the right ordering of the people of God. Therefore my neighbour stands before me not only as the object whereby I fulfil the law, but actually as my brother. Indeed the word *brother* plays a special role in Deuteronomy (xv.2 f., 7, 9, 11 f., xix.18 f. *et passim*). Now this means that the obligation to one's neighbour is one of love, not a particular commandment. Hence the law is again and again summed up in the command to love (vi.5, vii.9, x.12).

(*d*) But with all this, Deuteronomy endeavours to maintain at the same time also the distance between

---

[1] cf. O. Weber, *Bibelkunde des AT*, I (1935), p. 49.

[2] Thus e.g. von Rad (p. 36) draws attention to the fact that the ethical interest in the position of the country Levites is greater than in the means by which the cult is carried out in Jerusalem.

[3] This is the most important fresh conception in comparison with the Book of the Covenant. Cf. von Rad, pp. 14 ff.

God and man, not only in general terms because one
'partner' in the covenant is plainly the superior, but
also practically by combating the sub-moral worship
of God according to natural instincts. This is to be
achieved chiefly by the way the cult is ordered. So the
cult offering can be converted into money (xiv.24 ff.),
and it is not the act of propitiation which effects forgiveness, but the mercy of Yahweh (xxi.7 f.). The
centralisation of the cult too is not an irruption of
magical ideas, but the limitation of the cult to the
place chosen by God and hallowed by that fact alone
and not by man himself.

If thus the purpose of the law is to shape the people
to be the people of God, and to unite it to God alone,
in both cases because it has already been adopted by
God, then it is in the nature of things that the divine
blessing is promised when the law is kept. For this
blessing consists precisely in the full and untrammelled
enjoyment of that which is given to the people by its
God in its land, just as the curse for the contempt of
the law means the withdrawal of this gift.

In criticism of this, perhaps the most profound
attempt to understand God's OT covenant and to
fashion life by it, the OT attains also to the deepest
understanding of the nature of the law. In all prob-
ability this criticism is expressed in Jer. xxxi.31 ff.[1]
This exegesis assumes that Jeremiah concurred with
the Deuteronomic reform and its aims.[2] Yet Jeremiah
recognises that the weakness of this attempt lies in the
fact of sin by which the undisturbed relationship
between God and people is broken so that it cannot be
reconstituted by any law. Only the act of God in

[1] cf. von Rad, pp. 98 ff.

[2] Marti, pp. 182 f., 186 certainly explains many passages in
Jeremiah by reference to Deuteronomy in such a way as to make
it appear that he rejected it; yet this exegesis is often arbitrary.

creating the whole man anew and putting the law into his heart, and therefore only a new covenant of God, can guarantee the time of salvation. In this way Jeremiah points to something which is outside the scope of the OT revelation, but is fulfilled in the NT.

5. *The understanding of the law in the Priestly writings and related passages*

P differs characteristically from Deuteronomy in that he does not aim at influencing the reader by means of sermons for instruction, but propounds his material harshly and sternly in a tone which almost serves to discourage obedience.[1] This is probably not merely a difference of style, but is connected with a different conception of God, since in P, to an even greater extent than in Deuteronomy, the transcendent and absolute other-worldliness of God is the basis of all theological thinking. Besides, Deuteronomy's peculiar concept of the nation is not in the same way a controlling factor. In general P is not concerned with Israel alone, but takes mankind beyond Israel into consideration, even though the special position of Israel is nearest to his heart. But P regards the relationship of Yahweh to Israel not so much from the point of view of loving election, as from that of the rule of God set up to bring salvation. Now it is just here that in P the law has its theological place and its purpose. It protects the purity of the divine revelation by preserving God's otherness and ascendancy over the world. It is all the more significant that P aims at being a historical presentation, by no means for the purpose of edification but in order to demonstrate that God's action and therewith His revelation provides the justification and

[1] cf. von Rad, *Die Priesterschrift im Hexateuch* (1934), p. 187. For the following see also Eichrodt, *Theol.*, I, pp. 209 ff., ET pp. 392 ff. Also W. Eichrodt, 'Gottes ewiges Reich und seine Wirklichkeit nach alttestamentlicher Offenbarung', ThStKr 108 (1937), pp. 1-27.

D

obligation for the religious life of Israel, and indeed of the world. Thus he underlines the fact that the supramundane holy God is not an impersonal power, but a personal will.

The divine order established by God through His creative activity tells the individual and the nation how they can and should live, without forfeiting their existence by offending against the glory of God, the creator. By God's new revelation to Abraham, the people is appointed to be his possession. At Sinai the promise, implicit when the covenant was established, is fulfilled. In this way according to P, history shows how the ordinances which substantiate and safeguard the welfare of the people of God were manifested.[1] Thus the sovereignty of the God who creates and chooses expresses itself in the law and determines how the life of mankind—and especially of Israel—can be fitting for this holy God. This way of understanding the law provides the clue to the positive law in P.

In the tent of revelation (for the Tent of Meeting is in P characteristically the place where God appears, not where He dwells [Exod. xxv.22; Num. xiv.10]), Moses receives the ordinances and instructions for the people (Exod. xxv.22; Num. vii.89). In the will of God thus manifested, the standards of morals and of the cult have a deeper unity,[2] for both are testimony to God's dominion. The one regulates the relationship to one's neighbour, the other is a token of the intimate bond with God. This unity is expressed by the fact that Aaron acts only through Moses on the directions which the latter has received from God and handed on to him (Lev. xvi; Num. xvii.11 ff.). It is true that the cult is of great importance to P.[3] but it stands in this

---

[1] von Rad, *Priesterschrift*, p. 188.

[2] Eichrodt, *Theol.*, I, p. 228, ET p. 424.

[3] Apparently, indeed, to an increasing extent, as a comparison

whole framework of the revelation of the law to Moses. Consequently beside the cult, without any differentiation as to their value, we find the other ordinances of a legal and religious nature, which have been imposed and justified by history, as well as the moral standards in the narrower sense.

But this understanding of the law by no means excludes deep joy, humble and reverent worship, and selfless devotion. On the contrary P's description is itself evidence of this (cf. e.g. the story of the creation in Genesis i) and is thereby altogether in line with the tenor of the psalms of the law (e.g. Ps. xix, cxix). This removes P far from what is often called the religion of the law or Nomism on the basis of the NT hostility to Judaism.[1]

The Holiness Code (H) in Lev. xvii-xxvi also has an intimate relationship with P's view of the law. Here too man attains his highest worth by submitting himself to God's will. What differentiates this from P is not so much the stress laid on the moral obligation to one's neighbour (Lev. xix.15 ff., xxv.35 ff.), as the smaller extent to which the laws and institutions are justified by their history, although this latter aspect is not altogether lacking (Lev. xviii.1 ff.).

6. *Law in the post-exilic period*

The exile brought about a significant development in Israel's attitude to the law and consequently in the understanding of it. What the prophets had threatened had been fulfilled. Israel had fallen under Yahweh's judgement because it had been disobedient to him. So now after the return it becomes the predominant concern to carry out God's will. Israel must obey God's

of the two strands of the P tradition, demonstrated by von Rad *op. cit.* p. 163, enables us to see.

[1] cf. von Rad, *Priesterschrift*, p. 187, n. 34.

law in order to live. The exile had made this clear to the people.

To begin with this did not involve a change in the theoretical position of the law. The duty of keeping the law was still, indeed in a renewed sense, the result, not the basis, of their election. This applies to the presentation of history by the Chronicler and even to Ezra. His activity stands or falls by the certainty that God who is beyond the world has nevertheless chosen just this people for himself (Ezra ix.5 ff.).[1]

To fulfil the law does not create the relationship to God, but keeps unimpaired the existing one (cf. e.g. II Chron. xxxiii.8). Yet in fact the emphasis and passion are directed more and more to the second proposition that everything depends on the people's fulfilling the law. The transition to the later conception of the law according to which the relationship to God is first created by it is often not hard and fast. The law acquires an ever increasing independent importance, acquires a primary significance for the relationship to God. Besides the praise of what God did for their forefathers, the praise of the law for itself gains ever greater prominence (cf. too the two parts of Ps. xix) as being the God-given means for the nation by which it maintains itself in his favour.

(a) An important stage in the development of the law to its key position in the religious world of Judaism is the Deuteronomic and the Chronistic writing of history.[2] They both take for granted throughout the standard set by the law. Saul is rejected because he transgresses God's command. All the kings of Israel are judged from the point of view of the law. The throne of David is indeed guaranteed by God's promise, but yet in practice all depends on the law being kept

[1] cf. Schaeder.
[2] G. von Rad, *Das Geschichtsbild des chronistischen Werks* (1930).

(cf. e.g. II Chron. xxvii f.). The revision of the early historical material to be found in Judges describes this period according to the pattern: the nation sins, is penitent, appeals to God in its distress, God gives help by sending a deliverer, the nation sins anew (Judges ii.11 ff.). This presentation of history is prompted by the seriousness of the penitence which looks upon calamity as a just punishment for the violation of the divine will. This standpoint also leads, it is true, to the thought of guilt becoming unbearable in the case of periods and men in obvious enjoyment of God's favour. Chronicles passes over in silence David's sin and Solomon's fall. Nevertheless this writing of history brings home to the people that its existence is bound up with the keeping of the law. The prophets too are commandeered on behalf of the law and turned into its guardians and proclaimers (e.g. II Kings xvii.13).

(b) But it is not only this kind of historical writing which reveals the mounting importance of the law. It is seen just as much in the growing extent to which it is made the basis of the community's whole life.[1] This is the real meaning and purpose of Ezra's efforts (Ezra ix f.). Here too lies the point of departure for a continuous development, which has momentous consequences, but does not appear fully until later. From being a nation tied to the law Israel becomes a religious community gathered round the law.[2] To keep the law becomes the distinctive mark for membership of God's people. This begins to be of decisive importance for

[1] cf. E. Würthwein, *Der 'am ha'arez im AT* (1936), p. 66.

[2] cf. G. Kittel, *Die Religionsgeschichte und das Urchristentum* (1932), p. 69. Some of the Wisdom material clearly expresses this point of view, although as a rule 'wisdom' denotes a parallel movement which in the first instance has very little to do with the law.

the problem of the proselytes, just as on the other hand
this problem naturally fosters this inner development.

(c) In the cult too a reassessment is being prepared
for. It is becoming supremely important that the
divine service should be performed in conformity with
the law,[1] so that finally it came to be understood altogether solely—or at any rate primarily—as the carrying out of the law, and this conformity with the law
supplied not only the justification for the service, but
its whole meaning. So Jewry could later endure the
loss of the temple without a great shock to its religious
system.

(d) Finally, the new position of the law shows itself
in the fact that a new profession emerges to give religious guidance to the people (Ezra vii.10). Up till
then the priest was intended to administer the Torah;
but henceforward the study of the law becomes an
independent task which can be completely detached
from the priestly office.[2] The high esteem paid to the
scribes expresses the desire of the community to recognise the authority of the law alone, before which all,
including the priests, must bow.

All this need not mean[3] that casuistry becomes
dominant, that my neighbour as an individual person
disappears behind my fellow-man as the person
through whom I keep the law. It need not mean that
this obligation to observe the law is used for the secret
evasion of obedience, or as a guarantee against God.
That it need not mean this is evident from the genuine
piety of many psalms of this period (Ps. xix, xxxvii, xl,

---

[1] cf. e.g. the exclusion from the cult of those priests who cannot
prove their priestly descent with certainty (Ezra ii.62).

[2] cf. Eichrodt, *Theol.*, I, p. 214, ET pp. 400 f. Does II Chron.
xv.3 perhaps indicate a distinction in this sense between *tōrāh* and
the priests' teaching?

[3] cf. Kautzsch, pp. 352 f.; Schaeder, pp. 3 f.

cxix). But it can mean all this. With a certain inner conformity it did come to be all this in actual fact. And this illustrates the danger of this development, although its undoubted value is seen in the fact that to a large extent it really did create the will to subject oneself unreservedly to God's judgement and law.

7. The meaning of the word Torah

Amongst the various words in the OT which are used from time to time with different shades of meaning for 'law',[1] *tōrāh* is the expression which acquired the most comprehensive meaning and became predominant. In addition, through its translation in the LXX by νόμος, it has exerted greatest influence.

In the Hebrew text of the OT, *tōrāh* occurs about 220 times, with fairly wide differences of meaning. It does not occur in the J strand, in the E strand it occurs only seldom if indeed at all.[2] The earlier prophets use it rarely, but under certain circumstances with considerable emphasis. The Deuteronomic historical writings and Deuteronomy in its present form introduce it frequently. Similarly it is often found in the priestly laws, in the Chronicler's historical work, as well as in some of the Psalms.

For the understanding of the meaning of the word, nothing reliable can be gained from its etymology, even if this were established.[3] The only possibility is to

---

[1] cf. the survey in L. Köhler, *Theologie des AT* ([3]1953), 192 ff., ET *Old Testament Theology* (1957), pp. 203 ff.

[2] Exod. xiii.9, xvi.4, xviii.18, 20, xxiv.12 must be considered, but are open to question; though the doubts are perhaps least in xviii.16, 20. On xvi.4 cf. Procksch p. 203, n. 2.

[3] The customary derivation of the word from *yrh* to *throw*, to *cast the lot of the oracle*, has recently been contested by Begrich, pp. 68 f., cf. p. 69, n. 1, where nevertheless no detailed alternative explanation is given. [Cf. also G. Östborn, *Tōrā in the OT* (1945), ch. I.]

throw light on what is designated by *tōrāh* from those passages which are the earliest from the literary point of view and to proceed from there both forwards and backwards. Such passages testify to the administration of the Torah as the particular duty of the priest (Hos. iv.6; Zeph. iii.4; Mic. iii.11; also Jer. xviii.18; Ezek. vii.26, xxii.26). Yet Jer. ii.8 seems already to know of an administration of the law by persons other than priests.

But the earlier prophets also use *tōrāh* for the divine word proclaimed through them[1] (Isa. viii.16, cf. also v. 20; Isa. xxx.9 f.; perhaps also Isa. i.10). Besides this, certain passages in the earlier prophets use the word *tōrāh* also for the commandment of Yahweh which was written down: thus Hos. viii.12. Moreover these are clearly examples not only of ritual matters, but also of ethics.

Hence it follows that at any rate in this period *tōrāh* had the meaning of a divine instruction, whether it had been written down long ago as a law and was preserved and pronounced by a priest, or whether the priest was delivering it at that time (Lam. ii.9; Ezek. vii.26; Mal. ii.4 ff.), or the prophet is commissioned by God to pronounce it for a definite situation (so perhaps Isa. xxx.9).

Thus what is objectively essential in *tōrāh* is not the form but the divine authority. Normally it will at first have been a matter of actual cases which were decided by *tōroth*,[2] even though *tōrāh* can then too include a larger whole (e.g. Isa. i.10; and later Isa. ii.3; Mic. iv.2; Isa. xli.4, li.4, 7). At the same time, all this establishes the fact that in the usage of the early

---

[1] Jeremiah apparently does not. Perhaps in his case *tōrāh* has already become more definitely tied to the other type of meaning by the Deuteronomic movement.

[2] Köhler, *Theologie*, p. 195, ET p. 205.

prophets the word *tōrāh* docs not seem to convey any precise definition of its contents. Thus legal, cultic, political and other instructions can be designated as *tōrāh*, if they have divine authority. This simply corresponds to the basic understanding of the law ascertained above.

But beside this there is the fact that in some of the priestly corpora in Leviticus and Numbers *tōrāh* stands for the regulations concerning certain cultic and ritual procedures, at times attached to a small coherent section as a title or a colophon.[1] Possibly these statements are inserted so that these several instructions appear as parts out of the greater entity of the 'law',[2] but perhaps this too is only a later idea.

The meaning of *tōrāh* ascertained in the foregoing is carried on into later times in a twofold manner. Firstly *tōrāh* is still found subsequently too as the word for the cultic directions for the priest (Hag. ii.11; Mal. ii.6 ff.). At the same time, especially in Proverbs, *tōrāh* can have the general meaning of instruction.[3] Yet other parts of this collection of wisdom sayings use *tōrāh* only in the sense which became customary subsequently (Prov. xxviii.4, 7, 9, xxix.18).

The change in the meaning of *tōrāh* which became decisive for the future is brought about by the Deuteronomic writings. It is true that in the original Deuteronomy *tōrāh* seems still to be used in the old sense (Deut. xvii.11. It is often hard to distinguish, e.g. Deut. xxxii.46). Deuteronomy probably did not yet call itself 'the Torah'. But this happens already in the later

[1] Lev. vi.2, 7, 18, vii.1, 11, 37, xi.46; Num. v.29 f.; similarly no doubt Ezek. xliii.11 ff.

[2] There is e.g. a 'statute of the *tōrāh*' in Num. xix.2, xxxi.21; cf. Köhler, *Theologie*, pp. 195, ET, p. 206.

[3] Instruction by the mother in Prov. i.8, vi.20; or by the father in iv.2; the teaching of the sage in iii.1, vii.2. Perhaps Job xxii.22 belongs here as well.

strands and in the historical books which received the Deuteronomic imprint (II Kings xxii.8, 11). Now the individual instructions of the law are spoken of as *words of the tōrāh*, whilst up till then the plural *tōrōth* had been used.[1] Deuteronomy itself is a *book of the tōrāh* and when the king has to have a copy made of *this law*, then *tōrāh* is simply this law set down in writing (Deut. xvii.18 f.; Joshua viii.32).

As regards the content, usually *tōrāh* means Deuteronomy which is to be written on stones (Deut. xxvii.3, 8) and preserved with the ark (Deut. xxxi.26). According to the context, the Decalogue in particular may perhaps be meant (Deut. iv.44), but that is not normal. In this *tōrāh* are found not only laws. There are for instance the curses of the covenant (Deut. xxix, xxx). There are sicknesses and calamities which Yahweh can send and which are not recorded in this *book of the law* (Deut. xxvii.16; Joshua viii.34). This *book of the law* itself contains the explanation, namely that it inculcates the law with exhortations (Deut. i.5). Therefore to translate by 'law' restricts it too much. *Tōrāh* frequently has the general meaning of instruction, direction (cf. II Chron. xvii.9, xix.10; Neh. viii), even divine revelation as a whole (especially too in the Psalms: i.2, xix.8, xci.12). Nevertheless to use νόμος for its translation in the LXX is appropriate in so far as this *tōrāh* is after all *a parte potiori* an authoritative direction. This is confirmed by the fact that even earlier *tōrāh* was reproduced in Aramaic by *dáth* (law) which points in the same direction.[2]

[1] Gen. xxvi.5; Exod. xvi.28; Lev. xxvi.46; Ezek. xl.5; Ps. cv.45; probably also Deut. xxxiii.10 (cf. Begrich, p. 64, n. 9) and especially Exod. xviii.16, 20. Some of these passages are later; thus they show that in these matters there is no hard and fast rule.
[2] cf. Schaeder, p. 44; Ezra vii.12, 14, 25 f.; Esther i.8 ff., viii.12. *Dáth* is used of a royal decree, of public law, and of divine law in these biblical passages. Cf. below, p. 48.

In the works of the Chronicler and the later Psalms there is no further basic change in the use of *tōrāh*. But there is a change regarding its content, for now the whole of the Pentateuch is called *tōrāh*.[1] The principal names for this *tōrāh* are *tōrath Yahweh* (I Chron. xvi.40, xxii.12 *et passim*), *tōrath Moses* (II Chron. xxiii.18, xxx.16 *et passim*) or a combination of the two (II Chron. xxxiv.14; Ezra. vii.6 *et passim*), but *tōrāh* alone is now no longer ambiguous.

ADDITIONAL NOTE

νόμος *in the Septuagint*

In the LXX *tōrāh* is translated by νόμος in by far the largest number of cases (in about 200 out of 220). But compared with *tōrāh*, νόμος has been employed some- what more (c. 240 times). A change in the meaning of the word itself has resulted from the fact that νόμος in the LXX renders *tōrāh* at a later stage of its develop- ment and imposes this later meaning on other cases also. Thus for example in Isa. viii.16 what the prophet hands on to his disciples will probably, according to the LXX, have no longer been thought of as anything but the *Torah* in its later sense, that is to say the epitome of the divine teaching and the divine law. In other respects too a greater uniformity is attained by pushing into the background the earlier meanings of *tōrāh*. This occurs particularly in the conversion of old plurals of *tōrāh* into the singular νόμος (thus e.g. in Exod. xvi.28, xviii.16, 20; Isa. xxiv.5).

---

[1] For the books of Chronicles see the full index in von Rad, *Geschichtsbild*, pp. 38 ff. Also G. von Rad, 'Die Levitische Predigt in den Büchern der Chronik' in *Festschrift für O. Procksch* (1934), pp. 113 ff. (reprinted in *Gesammelte Studien* (1957), pp. 248-61). This is not intended to indicate that in these books the Pentateuch as we have it today is always meant.

Moreover the same is seen in those cases in which
tōrāh is not translated by νόμος. The changes can mostly
be explained by the fact that the Hebrew text contains
a meaning of *tōrāh* which does not agree with the main
trend of the post-exilic sense of νόμος and of *tōrāh*.
There are firstly again the cases of *tōrāh* in the plural
(Gen. xxvi.5; Prov. iii.1; Jer. xxvi.4 (LXX xxxix.23)).[1]
Here the LXX translates mostly with νόμιμα, once
with προστάγματα. Secondly there are cases where
tōrāh is an instruction given by human beings, as in
Prov. i.20, vi.20 (θεσμοί),[2] xxxi.26 (a paraphrase).
Lastly there are those cases where *tōrāh* means a single
instruction (II Chron. xix.10; Ezek. xliii.12).[3] But it
must be noted that the variations in this sense are by
no means carried through consistently; the cases
quoted show only the general shift in the meaning.

In addition to the rendering of *tōrāh* by νόμος in the
LXX, the extension of use of the latter to cover other
Hebrew terms does not produce a different picture.
This use consists firstly in the absorption of the Aramaic
terms *dāth* (c. 14 times) and *pithgam* (once). Next is the
assimilation of some passages which have *ḥōq* (statute)
(3 times) or *ḥuqqāh* (c. 12 times). The same can be said
of various small inconsistencies which individually do
not amount to anything of importance (c. 12 times) and

[1] It is true that in several of these passages the MT now has
the singular, but this is no doubt secondary.

[2] In Greek θεσμός is a rather more solemn word than νόμος.
Since in Judaism νόμος stands for *tōrāh*, there can be no more
solemn word than this.

[3] In these cases we must disregard simple errors, as e.g. in
Isa. xlii.21 where the LXX assumes *tōdāh* (praise, thanks) instead
of *tōrāh*; similarly in Job xxii.22 (cf. the opposite in Amos iv.5).
In some other cases we cannot see why the rule has not been
followed; thus e.g. in Deut. xvii.19; II Kings xxi.8 *et passim*. In
Deut. xvii.18; Joshua viii.32 the LXX understands the Hebrew
mišnē tōrāh (copy of the law) in the technical sense and so gives
τὸ δευτερονόμιον τοῦτο as the translation.

moreover in some cases the LXX has here a variant reading.

On the one hand, the aspect of the law prevailing in *tōrāh* in the later period won a complete victory and became predominant when *tōrāh* was replaced by νόμος. On the other hand, those elements in the meaning of *tōrāh* which reinforce the view of the law as teaching, instruction, revelation, have for their part been to a certain extent transferred to νόμος and this sometimes bursts through the limitations which this word derived from its earlier Greek usage.[1]

[1] For the relationship between νόμος and *tōrāh* cf. also C. H. Dodd, *The Bible and the Greeks* (1935), pp. 25 ff.

III. LAW IN JUDAISM

1. *Law in the Pseudepigrapha and the Apocrypha*

THERE is very little unity as regards content and language in the apocryphal and pseudepigraphical literature of Judaism. Nevertheless all these writings have a common bond in the matter of the law. In all of them the law is the foundation on which they rest.[1] Some of these writings are devoted to the law in particular; they are intended to inculcate it, to defend it, to praise it, and so forth. In the case of those dealing with other matters as well (as e.g. especially the apocalypses) the law is nevertheless of decisive importance.

(*a*) In the linguistic usage ὁ νόμος used absolutely has been widely accepted. This is not only true of the writings under Palestinian influence, as, for example, I Macc. where νόμος appears almost without exception absolutely and in the singular. It is true also in those books which are in other respects typical of Hellenistic Judaism, as for example the Letter of Aristeas (39, 122, 309). Besides this, νόμος appears as well without the article with no recognisable difference of meaning. *They turned away from the law of God* in Bar. iv.12 means simply that they have departed from God's Torah.[2] It is used in the same way in I Macc. iv.42 and especially frequently in Ecclus. (e.g. xix.20, 24, xxi.11 *et passim*).

Beside the predominant meaning of law in the sense of the imperative will of God, νόμος comes to stand

---

[1] cf. Bousset-Gressmann, pp. 119 ff.

[2] Nor is there here any question of a qualitative meaning when the word is used without the article (cf. below, p. 102, n. 3).

more and more for 'the Pentateuch', probably because
the law was felt to be the essential part of it. This
appears in the twofold formula *the law and the prophets*
in II Macc. xv.9; Ecclus. Prol. i.8 f., 24 (cf. also Zech.
vii.12 for the idea), and also in the more precise description *the book of the law* (I Esdras ix.45). It is also possible
to say 'he brought the law' when the book is meant
(I Esdras ix.39), 'the law is in one's hand' (Letter of
Aristeas 46). At the same time νόμος is used for the
book even when it is not to be understood as the actual
law. So II Macc. ii.17 f. is concerned with inheritance,
kingship and priesthood, and the consecration of the
people *as he* (sc. God) *promised through the law.* The
deeds of the Shechemites are written down in 'the
law' (Jub. xxx.12).

Naturally beside the absolute use there are found
the fuller expressions: *the law of the Lord* in I Esdras
i.33 *et passim*; *the law of God* in III Macc. vii.10, 12,
Test. Reuben iii; *the law of Moses*, I Esdras. viii.3, Tob.
vi.13 (MSS BA), vii.13 (MSS BA).

Other phrases are also used which are not derived
from a direct rendering of the Hebrew *tōrāh*. First of
all the plural οἱ νόμοι. Probably this is used for the
benefit of the Greek reader or it is an expression
familiar to the authors (I Macc. x.37, xiii.3; Additions
to Esther iii.13de, viii.12p; Judith xi.12; especially
II Macc. iii-x; Jub. *passim*). That this expression
definitely shows Greek influence is evident from other
phrases which are not found in the OT, but are
strongly reminiscent of Greek thought such as *to die for
their laws and their country*, II Macc. viii.21, xiii.10, 14.
Similarly expressions in a style alien to the OT are
found such as *the law of their fathers* in III Macc. i.23
et passim, *the laws of their fathers* in II Macc. vi.1, where
it is identical with *the laws of God*; also *the law of the
Most High* (Ecclus. xlii.2, xliv.20 *et passim*); *the divine law*

(Letter of Aristeas 3). But in all these cases no material change is involved. For instance II Macc. in particular, with its strictly Pharisaic attitude, shows no sign that the Jewish point of view concerning the law has been relaxed in favour of Greek influences. Seen as a whole the expressions characteristic of the OT are found also in those writings which in other respects are open to the Hellenistic spirit. Thus the Letter of Aristeas uses mainly the singular; in 111 alone the plural stands for the Jewish law, in 279 it is used in a more general sense.

(b) It should be observed that the content of the law, like the word itself, is understood in two ways. The position reached in the post-exilic OT period was firmly held, though certainly the outline was more sharply drawn in some respects. This took place partly through the continued development of legal thought itself, partly owing to historical events. In addition, new features were brought in by spiritual and intellectual influences from outside.

(i) What is strongly maintained in all this literature is the absolutely binding, divine force of the law. This is nowhere questioned, even in the Hellenistic-Jewish writings.[1] In the specifically Palestinian material, there is no sign of a substantiating of the validity of the law nor of real apologetics aimed at the apostate, which after all might be conceivable, for example, in view of the subject-matter of I Macc. God's law is eternally

[1] When in the Letter of Aristeas more cautious phrases seem occasionally to be used, this is probably to be attributed to the situation presupposed there, and not to the liberal opinion of the author, as when we read in 31: *the law which they contain, in as much as it is of divine origin, is full of wisdom and free from all blemish.* For the author himself, the law possesses divine validity even before it has been proved to be in accordance with reason, but this is not immediately true for the Gentile whose views he is here expressing.

valid; that is assured by its divine origin (Bar. iv.1; Jub. ii.33, vi.14 *et passim*).

Moreover the superiority of the law to all other religious activities becomes clearly apparent. The prophets inculcated the law (II Macc. ii.1 ff.; I Esdras viii.79 (EVV 82) *et passim*). The sacrificial worship of the temple makes sense only if the law is observed with the utmost care (Jub. xlix.15, l.11; Ecclus. xxxv.1 ff.; I Macc. iv.42 ff.). Indeed the law is more important than the temple, the learning of the scribe than the activities of the priests.[1] In the times of the Maccabees the various religious groups of the people gathered together to fight for the law and it was the question of the law which kindled the revolt (I Macc. i.41 ff.). It is particularly characteristic that, when it was no longer only a matter of freedom to carry out the law, but of political freedom as well, a strong group withdrew very definitely from the fight.[2]

This was the Pharisaic group, determined under all circumstances and whatever might be the consequences to adhere to the law and to the law alone. In fact the layman versed in the law becomes more and more the ideal of the pious person (cf. the description of him in Ecclus. xxxviii.24-xxxix.11).[3] The fact of apostasy within and proselytism without compelled it to be recognised that the religious classification of the individual was no longer fixed merely by his belonging to the Jewish nation, but only when his attitude to the law was known.

The historical circumstances of alien government and of the diaspora resulted in special value being

---

[1] cf. L. Couard, *Die religiösen und sittlichen Anschauungen der alttestamentlichen Apokryphen und Pseudepigraphen* (1907), pp. 141 f.

[2] cf. W. Förster, 'Der Ursprung des Pharisäismus', ZNW 34 (1935), pp. 35 ff.

[3] cf. Schaeder, p. 59, n.1.

E

placed on those parts of the law which distinguish the
Jew externally from other men, e.g. the Sabbath,
circumcision and the food laws. It is these points which
give rise to the struggle of the Maccabees. Apologetics
concerns itself primarily with these matters. Historical
writing establishes these laws particularly firmly (cf.
especially Jubilees).[1] The separation of the Jews from
the other nations is thus often regarded actually as the
purpose of the law.[2]

Above all the significance of the law and of keeping
the law for the condition of the individual and of the
nation is seen with ever greater distinctness. God's verdict, positive or negative, depends on the observance of
the law. The whole history of the people is set out even
more consistently than ever before from the point of
view of reward and punishment for the performance and
infringement of the law (I Esdras viii.81 ff. (EW 84 ff.);
Bar. iv.12; Prayer of Manasses). This is now carried
into explanations of externals, as in II Macc. xii.40,
where in the case of all who fell in a certain battle it
was ascertained that they wore charms *which the law
forbids the Jews to wear*, and then everyone realised that
this was the cause of their death. It is of course a great
support for this theory that the reward for keeping the
law can also be attained in the beyond.[3] Resurrection
will be the reward for faithful performance of the law
(II Macc. vii.9). Hence the law is the hope of the
pious in Syr. Bar. li.7; Test. Jud. xxvi. The pattern (performance of the law—reward, infringement of the law
—judgement) controls also to a large extent the eschatological and apocalyptic expectations for the
future, even when, as perhaps in Jub. i.23 ff., a complete fulfilment of the law is expected to come through

---

[1] At least two of these points are raised in the struggle over the
law in the days of early Christianity as well.

[2] cf. Couard, p. 142.   [3] Volz, *Eschatologie*, §§ 37 f.

the spirit. The keeping of the law is the decisive factor in God's verdict on man (and on the nation) and thus on their fate in this world and in the hereafter.

(ii) But there are also new features concerning the way the law is understood in this literature, arising chiefly out of its contact with the Hellenistic spiritual and cultural world. It is essentially an attempt at demonstrating that the law is true wisdom and its observance true reason. That the debate with Hellenism should take place so vigorously just around this question shows once again the preponderant importance of the law in the consciousness of the Jewish community. The Jewish parts of the Sybillines (chiefly books III-V), the Letter of Aristeas, III and IV Maccabees, the Wisdom of Solomon, Ecclesiasticus, all endeavour to bring about this synthesis of law and wisdom, of observance of the law and reason whether these books have a missionary or an apologetic trend.[1] Bar. iv.1: *She* (sc. Wisdom) *is the book of the commandments of God, and the law that endures for ever*. Ecclus. xv.1: *he who holds to the law will obtain her* (i.e. Wisdom). Piety based on wisdom had indeed already earlier become familiar in Judaism, but it can be accepted only if it can be combined with the piety of the law. In the canonical book of Proverbs the way is prepared for this by identifying the wise man with the righteous, the fool with the sinner. But now it is no longer enough to assert that they are identical. After all there were in fact passages in the law which could not at once be regarded as obviously reasonable and these were actually just those to which for other reasons particular

[1] Kautzsch, *Apokryphen und Pseudepigraphen*, xvi f.; Couard, 143, For the whole question of Judaism and Hellenism cf. W. Knox. 'Pharisaism and Hellenism' in *Judaism and Christianity*, II (1937); *idem, St. Paul and the Church of the Gentiles* (1939).

importance had to be attached.[1] The Letter of
Aristeas (130 ff.) is especially instructive for the
apologetic treatment of these questions, probably
already at the beginning of the second century B.C.[2]

On the other hand, the identification of wisdom and
law resulted also in the idea that strictly speaking all
men equally should keep the law. This is found at any
rate as an eschatological hope and becomes actually a
favourite idea of Hellenistic Judaism.[3] God's Torah,
like wisdom, becomes a universal law. Sib. Or. III 757
(cf. 719 f.) promises that *there will be one law in the
whole world*. The law is now no longer, as in the OT,
the rule of life for those belonging to the chosen people,
which they must lead because of their election. It is
now the timeless expression of the divine will with a
validity of its own.[4] We see the same trend when the
patriarchs before Moses are described as observing the
law with ever greater strictness. The reproach of being
without the law must not fall on them. This concern
is voiced especially clearly in Jubilees. Abraham
observed God's law (Jub. xxiv.11).[5]

Finally, at this point the idea of the law's pre-

[1] cf. pp. 53 f.

[2] cf. Schürer, III, pp. 608 ff. (4th ed.). ET (of 2nd ed, II.3,
pp. 308 ff.)

[3] Volz, p. 172. For the whole subject see W. Knox, *op. cit.*

[4] There is the further theory that the Gentiles knew God's law,
but had then rejected or forgotten it, without any need being felt
to demonstrate how this took place, IV Ezra iii.33 ff.; Syr. Bar.
xlviii.38 ff.

[5] It is true that in Jub. an occasional mention is made of the
fact that the law was not yet perfectly revealed before Moses'
time. Only since then has it become an eternal law for all races
of men (Jub. xxxiii.16). Accordingly there is sometimes an
allusion to a first law (ii.24, vi.22). It is of interest with regard to
Rom. ii.15 to note the way this idea is expressed in Syr. Bar.
lvii.2: the patriarchs performed the works of the commandments,
the law, though unwritten, was known to them.

existence is no longer distant. It is after all actually identical with divine wisdom which derives its existence and validity from itself.[1]

Thus the law has fully reached the position of intermediary between God and man, not only in practice, but also in theory. But this is now also the assumption underlying the hopelessness and despair arising out of the law, as seen in IV Ezra and Syr. Bar. There is no attempt at undermining the divine origin and the eternal validity of the law (IV Ezra iii.19, v.27, vii.8, 81, ix.36 f.), nor even the fact that the law bestows life on him who observes it (IV Ezra vii.21, xiv.30). But it is just this which takes away every hope of escape from a man who faces and takes seriously the actual transgressing of the law. For sin prevents the law bearing its fruit. IV Ezra iii.20: *thou didst not take away from them* (i.e. the patriarchs) *their evil heart, so that thy law might bring forth fruit in them.* It is just the knowledge of the law which makes sin grievous; vii.72: *though they received the commandments they did not keep them, and though they obtained the law they dealt unfaithfully with what they received.* Hence arises the lament in vii.46: *For who among the living is there who has not sinned, or who among those born who has not transgressed thy covenant?* and in ix.36: *we who have received the law, and sin, will perish.* It is to this that the Jewish understanding of the law leads when it is taken seriously.

2. *Josephus*

(a) In Josephus νόμος is used normally to designate the Jewish religious law; certainly the plural οἱ νόμοι also appears even more frequently, no doubt owing to his endeavour to speak good Greek and to be understood by readers trained in Hellenistic culture. Moreover in poetic language ὁ νόμος or οἱ νόμοι often become

---

[1] Couard, pp. 145 f.; Bousset-Gressmann, p. 121.

the subject of actions. The laws sigh in *Bell*. 3.356. The laws command in *Ant*. 16.3. Of course there can be no question of a personification of the law. νόμος without the article for the divine law is rare.[1] In other cases νόμος in Josephus is the OT or the Pentateuch: *a soldier, finding in one village a copy of the sacred law* (τὸν ἱερὸν νόμον), *tore the book in pieces . . .* in *Bell*. 2.229. *With a copy of Moses' laws* (τοὺς Μωυσέως νόμους) *in his hands . . .* in *Vit*. 134. Yet Josephus distinguishes between νόμος as the Pentateuch and the rest of the scriptures in *Ap*. 1.39.

But Josephus, when he does not mean the Jewish law itself, uses νόμος also for laws of other nations, sometimes even in comparison with the Jewish law (*Ap*. 2.172). There are also examples of military laws, cf. *Bell*. 5.123f. In addition, νόμος can be the prevailing custom without it being necessary to think that it was being raised officially to legal status, e.g. in *Ant*. 16.277 of the νόμος to avenge the murder of a kinsman. In this sense νόμος can be the custom, the rule, even what nature commands. There must be no grief for death *since undergoing it is in accordance with the will of God and by a law of nature* (φύσεως νόμῳ) in *Ant*. 4.322 (cf. *Bell*. 3.370, 374; also 5.367, 4.382). On the other hand Josephus does not identify this rule of nature with the Mosaic law, although they are not opposed to each other (*Ant*. 1.24), and although Josephus was for example impressed by the cosmic interpretation of certain regulations in the cult (*Ant*. 3.179 ff.).

There is still less Jewish feeling about the use of νόμος for the normal standard of a thing in *Bell*. 5.20: *the laws of history* (τῷ νόμῳ τῆς (συγ)γραφῆς) *compel one to restrain even one's emotions*: that which calls for the manner appropriate to the writing of history, the relevant, customary standard . . . (similarly *Bell*. 2.90).

[1] cf. Schlatter, *Theologie des Judentums*, p. 64.

But this usage of νόμος is rare in Josephus and in any case does not determine his understanding of the law.

(b) Just as Josephus' usage reveals his intermediate position, so also does his understanding of the nature of the law. In all essential matters his thought is Jewish, yet he enters very fully into the requirements of a cultured, non-Jewish reading public. The law has for Josephus the predominant position in religion.[1] The Jews are people who stress *the observance of our laws and of the pious practices based thereupon, which we have inherited* (*Ap.* 1.60). He admires those who set the observance of the law above all else (*Ant.* 11.152. The law controls the whole of life: *he* (i.e. Moses) *left nothing, however insignificant, to the discretion and caprice of the individual*; but for everything he gave the law as *standard and rule* (*Ap.* 2.173 f.; *Ant.* 3.94). At the same time the 'customs' are part of the law (*Ant.* 12.324; cf. *Ant.* 20.218, 13.297). This shows that Josephus belongs to the Pharisaic movement.[2] The circumcision demanded by the law and the acceptance of the law imply incorporation into Jewry (*Ant.* 13.257 f.); this means at the same time that the relationship of a man to God is brought about through the law. Hence Josephus is certainly not a mystic.

The reason for attributing this importance and authority to the law lies in its divine origin, which Josephus considers to be certain. *Such was the code of laws which Moses . . . learnt from the mouth of God and transmitted in writing to the Hebrews* (*Ant.* 3.286). To disobey the laws means therefore to disobey God (*Ant.* 20.44). Yet occasional more guarded ways of expressing himself are not lacking (*Ap.* 2.184). In particular he lays strong emphasis on Moses' function as a lawgiver. *Ant.* 3.266: *Moses would never have issued to his own*

[1] P. Krüger, *Philo und Josephus als Apologeten des Judentums* (1906), p. 20.   [2] Schlatter, p. 63.

humiliation statutes (i.e. the laws concerning leprosy) *such as these.* Moses tried to find a form of government in which God is the highest authority, i.e. the theocracy (*Ap.* 2.165). This praise of the lawgiver as a pious and wise man is obviously a concession to Greek ways of thought, especially if we add to this the argument that the excellence of the law is proved by its age (*Ap.* 2.279) and its unalterability (*Ap.* 2.184, 221; *Ant.* 20.218). The clearest pointer in this direction is the attempt to give a rational explanation and basis for the laws. For example, *Ant.* 2.274 is typical: the reason for forbidding adultery is that Moses believes that legitimate children are useful for the city and the house. Accordingly Josephus undertakes a work in which he plans to expound the *causes* (αἰτίαι) of the laws (*Ant.* 4.198 *et passim*). Of course the laws are not conceptions of human wisdom (*Ant.* 3.223), but nevertheless Josephus considers the endeavour worthwhile, perhaps to demonstrate by a comparison of the different laws and constitutions of the nations whose laws are the best (*Ap.* 2.163 ff.). Therefore Josephus considers it important that men in all countries should recognise the law (*Ap.* 2.284).

The two currents meet also when Josephus reflects on the purpose and aim of the law. It brings about a life pleasing to God (*Ant.* 3.213); but above all, and here Josephus' Pharisaic attitude again becomes evident, the law is intended to prevent sin: *the learning of our customs and law . . . so that we may not sin* (*Ant.* 16.43; cf. *Ap.* 2.173 f. The law makes it impossible to try to excuse sin by ignorance (*Ant.* 4.210). Moreover it is prized as the rule for public life. By giving the law God has *dictated for you rules for a blissful life and an ordered government* (*Ant.* 3.84). He who observes the law attains to blessedness. Adapting himself still more closely to Greek thought, Josephus can explain the law as enjoining the virtues, especially charity: *we possess a code excellently designed to promote piety, friendly relations with each other, and humanity towards the world at large, besides justice, hardihood, and contempt of death (Ap. 2.146: cf. Ap. 2.291; Ant. 16.42).*[1]

In his consideration of the motives for keeping the law Josephus follows on the whole the customary lines. Fear of punishment and hope of rewards play their part (*Ant.* 3.321, 4.210, 6.93 *et passim*). But he emphasises above all the fact that the Jews have the law impressed upon them at an early age (*Ap.* 2.178; cf. *Ant.* 4.211; *Bell.* 7.343). For him the importance attached to the Jews' practical training in the law is a main reason why it is superior to the laws of other nations (*Ap.* 2.172, 20.44). But with his eye upon apologetics he once again emphasises the fact that in Judaism it is a matter of observing the law joyfully and willingly. What is most clearly seen is *our voluntary obedience to our laws (Ap.* 2.220). Indeed it is his conscience which drives the Jew to fulfil the law (*Ant.* 3.319).

Thus Josephus' understanding of the law is seen on the one hand to be based in its essential content on Jewish, and indeed on Pharisaic, thought; but on the other hand a considerable adjustment has also been made, probably with apologetics primarily in view, to the rationalistic and moralistic world of Hellenistic thought.

3. *Philo of Alexandria*

(*a*) In his linguistic usage of νόμος, Philo does not differ essentially from Josephus. ὁ νόμος and νόμος are normally the Torah of the Palestinians. The *humanity*

---

[1] It is true that Josephus stresses the fact that these virtues are all rooted in piety: *for he* (i.e. Moses) *did not make piety a department of virtue, but the various virtues . . . departments of piety (Ap.* 2.170 f.).

of the law (Spec. Leg. 2.138), for example, is the love for one's fellowmen enjoined by the OT law. There are *exhortations to piety* διὰ τῶν νόμων *(Deus Imm.* 69). But the law of a state can equally well be called οἱ νόμοι. *Now in a democracy, physicians are represented by laws,* in *Jos.* 63, is of quite general application. Gentiles too have a *law against adultery (Vit. Mos.* 1.300). Yet ὁ νόμος is also the Pentateuch. The law says that the quantity of corn amassed by Joseph could not be counted *(Poster. C.* 96). In *Abr.* 1 he writes that the sacred laws are written down in five books. Indeed a single saying from the Scriptures can apparently be called νόμος even if it is not in the nature of a command: *in the laws ... (laws, that is, in the proper sense of the word) ... there are two leading statements, one that 'God is not a man'* (Num. xxiii.19); *the other that 'He is as a man'* (Deut. i.31) *(Deus Imm.* 53).

Philo gives a far wider range of meaning than Josephus to νόμος as an ordinance and law of nature (ὁ τῆς φυσέως νόμος, *Abr.* 135), and moreover in a twofold meaning (though these two can often hardly be distinguished): (i) as a law of nature: it is *nature's incontrovertible law* that what has come into being ranks below the producer of it *(Plant.* 132); (ii) as an ordinance: Laban does not observe *the true laws of nature (Ebr.* 47). Indeed something can be written *on the tables of nature (Spec. Leg.* 1.31), just as something else is written *on the most holy tables of the law (Op. Mund.* 128).

Philo also uses νόμος for the standard assigned to and appropriate for a particular sphere or subject, as in *the laws of perfect music (Op. Mund.* 70.54; *Omn. Prob. Lib.* 51); *according to the laws of allegory (Abr.* 68).

Finally in a figurative sense a person can be an embodiment of the law. In *Vit. Mos.* 1.162, we read that before Moses became a lawgiver he was *the reasonable and living impersonation of law.* The life of

Abraham was not only a *life obedient to the law* (νόμιμος),[1]
but *himself a law and an unwritten statute* (*Abr.* 276; cf.
Abr. 8).

(*b*) It will hardly be possible to give an objective and
consistent account of Philo's statements about the law
and the way he understood it; for the real centre of his
religious thought is not the law nor the necessary
religious feeling with regard to the law. His fundamental religious and philosophical attitude is that of a
mystical ecstatic; the highest level of religion for him
is contemplative oneness with the deity, to dwell in
solitude in the otherworldly realm of wisdom (*Spec.
Leg.* 3.1).[2] From this central position he can have only
an indefinite outlook upon the law of the OT; indeed
he probably ought really to renounce it. But this he
cannot do, and more particularly this he does not wish
to do. On the contrary he desires to cling to the sole
authority of the divine law, for he is and remains a
Jew.[3]

This dichotomy between the presuppositions which
he cannot give up and the actual theological and
philosophical mainspring of his existence, explains also
what he says about the law.

In Philo's treatment of the law, his crucial concern
is to prove the congruity between the OT law and the
ordering of the world as a whole by reason and nature.
For him this is an extremely personal question, and
he is no doubt influenced by an interest which is not
simply apologetic.

Moses gave the law, *holding that the laws were the most
faithful picture of the world-polity* (*Vit. Mos.* 2.51). *What
else are laws and statutes but the sacred words of nature?*

---

[1] cf. also below, p. 143.

[2] Krüger, p. 57; Bousset-Gressmann, pp. 443 f., 449 f.

[3] Schürer, III, p. 700. ET II.3, pp. 36 f, 364 f. Another reason
for the lack of consistency in Philo is the variety of his sources.

(*Spec. Leg.* 2.13).[1] He sees the strongest evidence for
the harmony between law and reason, world-order and
nature, in the oneness of God; in this, creation and
revelation are one. In *Vit. Mos.* 2.48 Moses shows *that
the Father and Maker of the world was in the truest sense also
its Lawgiver*. The order of events in the Pentateuch,
which records the creation of the world before the
giving of the law, offers him the proof of this.

Moreover Philo uses Israel's patriarchs to demonstrate this harmony. For without knowing the revealed
law, they live nevertheless in complete harmony with
it.[2] Indeed they are its embodiment, they are the unwritten law (*Abr. passim*). They practice the law by
nature; therefore natural reason and the revealed law
are in harmony.

This does not mean that Philo wishes to deny the
supernatural origin of the law. In *Decal.* 15 he says
that *the laws were not the inventions of a man but quite
clearly the oracles of God.* God himself made the Decalogue known in a miraculous way without human
agency (*Decal.* 10). On the contrary all this merely
corresponds with the other proposition that man can
after all never raise himself by his own strength into the
world of the deity.[3]

In order to demonstrate that this basic concern of
both theology and philosophy has a concrete and consistent application, and that nature and revelation,
philosophy and the law, are in agreement, the allegorical interpretation of the law is required.[4] Philo

---

[1] In contrast to this, the laws of the other nations are not in
the same way the authentic expression of the natural order, but
are additions to it (Philo, *Jos.* 31).

[2] This is a self-evident axiom which requires no further proof,
cf. p. 56.   [3] Schürer, III, p. 714. ET II.3, p. 379.

[4] E. Stein, *Die allegorische Exegese des Philo aus Alexandrien*,
BZAW 51 (1929); *idem, Philo und der Midrasch*, BZAW 57 (1931).

certainly allows the literal meaning also to have its rightful place, but a further step is necessary *to allegorical interpretations (Conf. Ling.* 190). *Let us rather in obedience to the suggestions of right reason expound in full the inward interpretation (Sobr.* 33).

It is true that Philo defends himself against those who neglect to keep the commands because of such an allegorical exegesis, and he maintains on the contrary that they impose an obligation even in their literal sense (*Migr. Abr.* 89). But this reasoning, which objectively is very weak, merely reveals that this opinion does not arise as the logical consequence of his premise, but is an inconsistency to be attributed to his Jewish way of thinking.

Beside the allegorical treatment of the law, there is in Philo a scientific one. This differs in its method from the former, but in the last resort it proceeds from the same need. It takes the form firstly of unifying and systematising the legal material, and then giving the laws a reasoned explanation, especially those laws which make a distinction between Jew and Gentile.[1] In both cases Philo succeeds in placing in the background or removing what is offensive when brought forward for judgement before the standards of speculative reason and of universal ethics.[2] Here it is likely that there is operative a more definite intention to introduce apologetics. In consequence we cannot fail to recognise a striking agreement with Josephus or even with the Letter of Aristeas. But here too Philo shows sufficient characteristics of his own. The whole law can be traced back to one simple requirement: *But among the vast number of particular truths and principles . . . there stand out . . . two main heads: one of duty to God*

[1] cf. pp. 53 f.

[2] This tendency is especially marked when Philo calls the law the preacher and teacher of virtuous behaviour (*Virt.* 119).

as shewn by piety and holiness, one of duty to men as shewn by humanity and justice, each of them splitting up into multiform branches, all highly laudable (*Spec. Leg.* 2.63; cf. *Spec. Leg.* 1.300). The Decalogue in particular is the summary of the whole legislation, the foundation for everything else. The purpose of systematising and harmonising is to enable the legislation to be grasped by reason, a typically Hellenistic concern.[1] The rational basis given for the individual commandments follows the same lines; for example circumcision is presented in *Spec. Leg.* 1.3 ff. by means of a number of hygienic and theological and allegorical considerations as the only correct course of action.

Finally as regards the manner in which the law achieves its object, Philo emphasises in particular its liberal nature. It encourages more than it commands. In *Vit. Mos.* 2.51 he says: *In his commands and prohibitions he* (i.e. Moses) *suggests and admonishes rather than commands, and the very numerous and necessary instructions which he essays to give are accompanied by forewords and afterwords, in order to exhort rather than to enforce.* It is certainly important to inculcate the law by reading it and meditating on it daily (*Spec. Leg.* 4.161). But basically the perfect man does not need to be admonished by the law. In *Leg. All.* 1.93 f. he says: To the perfect man the law is not something outside himself, alien to him; it is natural for him to act in accordance with divine reason and wisdom, and the law is simply the expression of these. Therefore it is not really an arduous matter to observe the law.

All this shows that Philo bears witness to the veiled, though actually unmistakable, disintegration of the law in favour of Hellenistic speculation and ethics, a disintegration brought about by allegorical exegesis, scientific

[1] Similar features amongst the rabbis and in the NT have a different motive (cf. below).

reasoning and the reconciliation of moral principles, as well as by the preservation of the practice of the law.[1]

4. Law in Rabbinic Judaism

The expression used to designate the whole of what the rabbis understood as the law is *tōrāh*. The rabbinic *tōrāh* is at the same time in most cases the equivalent of the NT νόμος.

(a) The usage of *tōrāh* in rabbinic writings is at the start the same as at the end of the OT period. Nevertheless it had been subjected in the interval to characteristic developments.

Torah is primarily the whole of the Mosaic law regarded as law (the following section contains references). This is the foundation of all the other meanings of the word *tōrāh* in the rabbinic literature. Thus *tōrāh* can certainly be used in particular for the Decalogue, but the Decalogue is never by itself the Torah. 'The ten commandments ought really to be recited daily; and why are they not recited? Because there is no wish to provide a basis for the assertions of heretics, so that they cannot say that these alone were given at Sinai (are divine)' (j Ber. 3c 32 f.).[2]

Beside the meaning of Torah as the Mosaic law, Torah stands just as often for that part of the OT canon which contains this law, i.e. the Pentateuch.[3] In most

---

[1] However arresting may be the resemblance of Philo's attitude to the law to that of the OT, yet in essentials the gulf is very great, for they each start from a completely different point. Consequently the fact that in the Early Church Christian criticism accepted and understood the law in Philo's way (cf. Epistle of Barnabas) had important consequences.

[2] J. Wohlgemuth, 'Das jüdische Religionsgesetz in jüdischer Beleuchtung', *Beilage zum Jahresbericht des Rabbinerseminars in Berlin* [1921], p. 21.

[3] For the following cf. the discussion of Canonical and Apocryphal works in TWNT III, pp. 979 ff..

cases it is difficult to discriminate between Torah as
'Law' and Torah as the Pentateuch. Yet the Pentateuch is called Torah in those cases also where there is
no question of the legal nature of its contents. (References from the Torah = Pentateuch: S Deut. 1 on i.1;
47 on xi.21; TBM 11.23; b Taan. 9a). This normal
usage of Torah can then also be extended to indicate
all the writings of the OT, because these other writings
are in harmony with the Torah, and derive their
whole authority simply from their agreement with
the Torah. In S Deut. 54 on xi.26, Ps. xxxiv.14, Prov.
xvi.4 are introduced by the set phrase *the tōrāh states*.
In M Ex. 15.8 references for the proposition of the
school of Ismael: 'There is no earlier or later in the
Torah' are given in passages from Isaiah, Jeremiah,
Hosea.[1] The juxtaposition of Torah in its wider and
narrower senses is illustrated particularly well in
Tanch. 10 (ed. Horeb 123b): 'the Torah (i.e. the OT)
contains Torah (i.e. Pentateuch), Prophets and
Writings'.[2]

Moreover in a particular context, Torah can have
the still more extended meaning of authoritative
teaching in general. Tradition as distinct from the
Scripture is called *tōrāh which is upon the mouth*.[3] In this
most extended sense of Torah it is often not appropriate
to translate it by 'law'. It has here rather the more
general meaning of *authoritative teaching*, *revelation*,
although the person's action which this Torah regulates is always the first consideration. Therefore there
can be only one Torah. Thus the plural *tōrōth* occurs

---

[1] W. Bacher, *Die exegetische Terminologie der jüdischen Traditions-
literatur*, I (1884, ²1903), II (1890): I, pp. 167 ff.

[2] W. Bacher, *Die Agada der Tannaiten*, I (²1903), p. 476.

[3] *tōrāh šebeʿal pe*. W. Bacher, *Tradition und Tradenten in den
Schulen Palästinas und Babyloniens* (1914), pp. 22 ff. gives passages
and basic material.

merely so to say *per negationem*; as for example when it is said that the difference between two schools is so great that one might suppose the Torah had broken into two Toroth (b Sanh. 80b).

Finally, Torah can have the special sense of 'Study of the .Torah', particularly when contrasted with *miṣwah (commandment)* meaning 'fulfilment of the law'. Thus according to Ex r 31 on xxii.26 the study of the Torah[1] is inseparable from the fulfilment of the law and vice versa. b Sota. 21a[2]: 'A transgression nullifies [the merit of] a commandment but not of [study of] Torah.' Indeed the study of the Torah is occasionally placed above obedience to the commandments.

(b) As regards its subject-matter, the way rabbinic Judaism understood the law can be summed up in two propositions which are in fundamental accord with each other: (1) God revealed himself once for all in the Torah and in the Torah alone; (2) man's relationship to God exists only through his relationship to the Torah. Thereby the basic starting point of the OT which can be summarised in the propositions: God revealed himself to Israel as its God, therefore Israel owes obedience to this God, is characteristically and decisively altered and invalidated. In theory, it is true, both these propositions remain in force, but in

[1] Wohlgemuth, p. 77, n. 1.

[2] Shab. 30a is a particularly interesting passage: 'As soon as a man has died he is released from the Torah and the commandments.' This sentence appears at first sight to be a parallel to Rom. vii.1. But it is preceded by: 'Let a man be always occupied with the Torah and the commandments before he dies; for when he has died the Torah and the commandments will have ceased for him, and the Holy One, blessed be He, will no longer be praised by him.' This makes it evident that here 'Torah' must mean the study of the law, and 'commandments' obedience to the commandments. Thus the parallel to Rom. vii.1 falls to the ground.

F

fact the Torah forces itself right into the foreground and indeed primarily as the law laying claim to men's will.

(i) The central and dominating position of the Torah as the law contained in the Pentateuch is seen already in the dependent relationship in which all the other sections, authoritative in some measure, stand with regard to the Torah. This is of course the implicit assumption in the extension of the concept of the Torah just described. The rest of the OT writings contain basically nothing different from the Pentateuch; at the very least everything must be anticipated in it. At any rate they only possess authority if this agreement is present. For instance the only reason why Koheleth (Ecclesiastes) was not withdrawn from use was because 'it begins with the words of the Torah and ends with the words of the Torah' (b Shab. 30b).[1] This view is expressed characteristically in the name *qabbālāh* (*tradition*) given to the writings of the OT not included in the Pentateuch.[2] These writings too are valid because they are 'Sinaitic' (cf. (ii) below), though they were only fixed later. This part of the OT explains and inculcates the law, but is not in itself absolutely necessary. 'If Israel had not sinned, he would have been given only the five parts of the Torah and the book of Joshua' (b Ned. 22b). On principle there is the same relationship also between the written and the oral Torah. In the case of the latter it is at first a tacit assumption that it agrees with the Torah. But after about the time of Johanan ben Zakkai,[3] the

[1] Moore, I, pp. 246 f. For a more detailed discussion cf. TWNT III, p. 985.

[2] Bacher, *op. cit* (p. 68, n. 3) pp. 2 f.

[3] N. Glatzer, *Untersuchungen zur Geschichtslehre der Tannaiten* (1933), p. 5. See also R. Herford, 'The Law and Pharisaism', in *Judaism and Christianity*, Vol. III, edited by E. Rosenthal (London 1938).

practice of establishing the exegesis of traditional material firmly on the Torah was carried through in accordance with definite exegetical methods. What could not be fitted in was considered to be *halākāh* given to Moses at Sinai.[1] Actually the theory that the traditional material originated in the exegesis of the Torah is of course artificial. It has dogmatic, not historical, validity. But the theory demonstrates how forcibly this concept of the law has taken control of all the other parts of authoritative doctrine, since they maintain their authority only in so far as they can be understood as exegesis or elaboration or even reconstruction[2] of the Torah.

(ii) The authoritative nature of the law is preserved by adhering strictly to the direct divine origin of the Pentateuch.[3] So b Sanh. 99a: 'If a man says that the whole Torah came from heaven with the exception of this verse which was said not by God, but by Moses out of his own mouth, then it is true to say of him: he has despised the word of Yahweh'. Here too is the right place for the peculiar assertion that all valid doctrine, every recognised rabbinic tenet, every accepted conclusion of exegesis was revealed to Moses on Sinai.[4] This theory undoubtedly springs from the desire to show that revelation at Sinai took place once for all and was a unity because of its all-embracing divine nature. Thus it is a judgement of faith, not a historical theory, and so it is naturally not maintained in many non-essential cases. In b Pes. 54a it is stated that the Torah is one of the seven things which were created before the world came

---

[1] Bacher, *op. cit.* (p. 68, n. 3), pp. 21 f., 33 ff. S. Kaatz, *Die mündliche Lehre und ihr Dogma* I (1922), II (1923), II, pp. 1 ff.

[2] Kaatz, II, p. 5.

[3] Pesikt. r 22; 111a, Strack-Billerbeck, IV.438. For the age of this view cf. Philo (see p. 64).

[4] Kaatz, I, pp. 130 ff.

into being.[1] Because the Torah is more precious than
anything else, it was created before all else (referring
to Prov. viii.22) : S Deut. 37 on xi.10.[2] Hence the Torah
is handed to Moses in a finished form. He himself plays
a completely passive role. He is an agent; the Torah
is given to him in writing or dictated to his pen or even
taught him by word of mouth,[3] but he is never regarded
as its spiritual originator.[4] Moses' sin, on account of
which he is punished, is written down 'so that it cannot
be said that it seems that Moses made false statements
in the Torah, or that he said something which he was
not ordered to say' (to which his punishment might
otherwise be ascribed) (S Deut. 26 on iii.23). Therefore when the Torah is copied, it is as if a world were
to be destroyed if one letter more or less is written
down (b Sota 20a). Moreover the sacredness of the
Torah finds expression in the tenet that the sacred
writings defile the hands (i.e. make it necessary to wash
them before a profane occupation), Yad, 3.5 *et passim*.
This sacredness gives to the study of the Torah its pre-
eminent dignity. God says to David: 'I prefer one day
during which you sit and concern yourself with the
Torah rather than 1000 burnt sacrifices which your son
Solomon will one day offer me upon the altar' (b Shab.
30e).

(iii) This divine authority of the law is also the basis
of the reticence shown by the rabbis—apparently to

[1] Not eternal pre-existence, against F. Weber, *Jüdische Theologie*
([2]1897), p. 15. The Torah too was created, though first of all.
This must be affirmed all the more strongly in consideration of
the fact that the pre-existence of the Torah probably arose
because the same value was placed in Hellenistic Judaism on the
Torah as on the principles of world-order.

[2] For further passages and details cf. Strack-Billerbeck, II,
pp. 353 ff.   [3] Strack-Billerbeck IV, p. 439.

[4] The wisdom of the law is never attributed to the wisdom of
Moses, as it is for example in Philo and Josephus.

an increasing extent—towards the questions concerning
the *ṭaʿᵃmē hattōrāh*, the *reasons* (the αἰτίαι cf. Jos.) for
the Torah. Johanan ben Zakkai says: 'By your life,
the dead man does not defile nor does water cleanse,
but it is an ordinance of the All Holy, the reasons for
which must not be sought out' (Pesikt. 40a). Thus for
example they refuse to derive from God's compassion
the prohibition to slaughter the female animal and her
young on the same day (j Ber. 9c 20 ff.). No doubt this
again is only the basic theoretical attitude intended to
meet the danger of superficiality.[1] For in practice
finding reasons for the commandments is a favourite
device for showing acumen and it is employed for
edifying purposes.[2] But there is no real concern behind
this, particularly no apologetic concern. There is no
intention of bringing out the real meaning of the law
by means of a standard lying outside the law itself.
Argument is consciously avoided in the case of just
those laws for which reasons are often given in the
apologetics of Hellenistic Judaism and in discussions
with Gentiles.[3]

(iv) The precise and consistent working out of the
authoritative nature of the Torah is carried so far that
God himself is conceived as tied to the Torah, studying
it and observing it, b AZ 3b: 'During the first three
hours of the day God sits and occupies himself with the
Torah'. Of course this must not be taken in a dogmatic
sense, but as a more or less poetical expression. Yet it
is a characteristic indication of the position of the
Torah towering above everything else, to which God
has committed himself wholly and completely.[4] The

[1] Strack-Billerbeck, III, p. 398.
[2] Wohlgemuth (pp. 39 ff.) produces a large number of examples; for the principle involved, *ib*. pp. 30 ff.
[3] Examples in Wohlgemuth, pp. 71 f.
[4] Wohlgemuth, pp. 80 ff.; Weber, pp. 17 ff., 159 f.

Torah is therefore eternally valid; R. Johanan (c. 250) can say 'Prophets and scriptures will come to an end, but not the five books of the Torah' (j Meg. 70d, 60).

Even the Messiah does not, it seems, bring a new Torah. On the contrary he will himself study and observe it, possibly he will also teach the reasons for it.[1] He will bring apostates back into submission to the Torah[2] and will impart at least a part of the law to the Gentiles.[3] He receives the promises due to him because he occupies himself with the Torah (Midr. Ps. ii.9).

All this establishes the Torah as the one and only mediator between God and man, indeed between God and the world. 'When two are sitting together and they occupy themselves with the words of the Torah, then the Shekinah dwells amongst them' (Ab. 3.2). 'Usually when a man buys something valuable in the market, is it possible for him to acquire its owner at the same time? But God has given the Torah to Israel and has said to them: "It is as though you are receiving Me" ' Ex. r 33, 7 on xxv.2 (towards the end).

(v) All other relationships between God on the one hand and man, Israel, or the world on the other, are subordinated to the Torah. 'It is the instrument with which man was created' (Ab. 3.14; S Deut. 48 on xi.22). When creating the world God took counsel with the Torah; it is the overseer for every act of creation.[4] Indeed the world, man and Israel are brought into being for the sake of the Torah alone (Gn. r on i.1 (towards the beginning); Ab. 3.14; M Ex. xiv.29). History too is fitted with complete consistency into the

---

[1] e.g. Tg. Cant. viii ff.; Strack-Billerbeck III, pp. 570 f.

[2] e.g. Tg. Is. liii.11b, 12; Strack-Billerbeck I, pp. 482 f.

[3] e.g. Midr. Ps. xxi.8 (89a).

[4] Thus the relationship assigned to creation and revelation by the rabbis and indirectly expressed here is completely subjected to the supremacy of revelation (unlike Philo, for example).

pattern of the law, its violation or its observance. Thus the Torah holds the key position in the whole religious life of rabbinic Judaism.

(vi) The Torah has therefore the power to sort men out into their order among themselves. Israel and the Gentiles are distinguished essentially according to whether or not they possess the law. It has indeed been given to all nations in seventy languages (b Shab. 88b) or at least it has been offered to them,[1] but they have not accepted it or at any rate they do not carry it out (S Deut. 343 on xxxiii.2). R. Meir (c. 150) said, though without the approval of the majority, that even a Gentile who occupies himself with the Torah should receive the same esteem (or respect) as the high-priest. He finds evidence for this in Lev. xviii.5, by emphasising: 'by doing this a man shall live' (b Sanh. 59a). In the same way individuals belonging to Israel are differentiated according to their knowledge of the Torah and their attitude towards it. This is the origin of the important position held in the community by the man learned in the law. If a man learns both the Scripture and the Mishnah, but has not served under a wise man (as a pupil) he is considered to be 'am hā'āreṣ.[2] He who has learned merely the Scriptures without the Mishnah is considered a bōr (uneducated person). But of him who has learned neither the Scripture nor the Mishnah, such words as those in Prov. xxiv.20 may be used (b Sota 22a).

(vii) Now it is the purpose of the law to show a man what he should do, or leave undone, as the case may be.[3] By this means, because he obeys the law, he

---

[1] For further details, including ideas concerning the manner in which this was done, see Strack-Billerbeck, III, pp. 38 ff.

[2] [Literally 'people of the land', but employed in this technical sense.]

[3] The negative side, not to transgress a command, carries

possesses God's approbation, righteousness and so life
itself, and a share in God's future world. 'Why has
God given us commandments? Is it not that we may
perform them and receive a reward?' (S Nu. 115 on
xv.41). R. Hananiah ben Akashya (c. A.D. 150) said:
'God wished to let Israel earn many merits; therefore
he gave much Torah and many commandments, as it
is written: "It pleased Yahweh, in order to bestow
merit on him (Israel) to make the Torah great and
mighty" ' (thus Isa. lxii.21 according to the Midrash).[1]
The Torah therefore signifies life. As food maintains
the life of the fleeting hour, so the future life is contained in the Torah (M Ex. xiii.3). R. Simeon (c.
A.D. 150) said: 'God speaks thus to man: "My Torah
is in thy hand and thy soul is in my hand; if thou
keepest what is mine, I will keep what is thine; if thou
destroyest what is mine, I will destroy what is thine." '
(Dt. r 4.4 on xi.26). For one the Torah is the spice of
life, for another the spice of death (b Yoma 72b).
Transgression of the Torah does not destroy the Torah
itself, but its transgressor (Lev. r 19 on xv.25).

Now of course the obligation to observe the Torah
can also be regarded from the point of view that it
involves man in danger of death and condemnation.
Just as the Torah became disastrous to the Gentiles,
because they could and indeed should have learned it,
but did not learn it (b Sota 35b), so there are also
voices speaking for Israel among the Rabbis who are
dismayed at the difficulty of keeping the law completely. 'As R. Gamaliel (II) read this verse (Ezek.

greater weight with the rabbis than the fulfilment of the positive
commands. In discussion what is forbidden is usually laid down
much more precisely than what is commanded. The righteous
man is praised for his avoidance of sin even more than for his
knowledge of the law (b Shab. 31b).

[1] Strack-Billerbeck, IV, p. 6; Bacher, *Tannaiten*, II, p. 376.

xviii.9) he wept and said: "He who performs all this, is righteous; but alas, not he who performs only one of these".' It is true that Akiba referring to Lev. xviii.24a then says to him that on the contrary even one is sufficient (b Sanh. 81a).[1] On the whole the view that it is possible on principle to fulfil the law is firmly maintained; that is in fact an inner necessity. At least it is asserted that certain individuals were completely sinless. 'We find that Abraham, our father, kept the whole Torah before it had been given' (Kid. 4.14).[2]

(viii) The fact that life depends on fulfilling the Torah makes it a very important concern that the law should be developed in the direction of case-law. The law and its development and practice support the religious existence of the Jew. Yet this is not to say that only the casuistical obedience to the individual commandments and prohibitions was regarded as a proper fulfilment of the law, however predominant this obedience may be.[3] There are other statements which name sincere piety and fear of God as the

[1] cf. for this whole question M. Löwy, 'Die paulinische Lehre vom Gesetz', MGWJ NF 11 (1903), pp. 322 ff., 417 ff., 534 ff.

[2] cf. further Strack-Billerbeck, III, pp. 186, 204 f. This idea is old, cf. p. 56. Philo's interest in it cannot be seen amongst the rabbis.

[3] The rabbis do indeed take note occasionally of a summary of the law in one or several main commandments. But this summary, as too the distinction between superficial and serious commands (cf. Wohlgemuth, pp. 13 f.), has no fundamental importance. In b Shab. 31a the story is told of a Gentile who asked Hillel if he could tell him the Torah whilst standing on one foot. So Hillel answered: 'Do not do to your neighbour what you do not like for yourself. That is the whole law; everything else only explains it. Go and learn it.' David reduced it to 11 (commandments), . . . Isaiah to 6, . . . Micah to 3, . . . Amos to 1 (Amos v.4), Habakkuk to 1 (Hab. ii.4) (Mak. 23b/24a). Yet basically one law is worth as much as any other, and statements like this are playful and edifying rather than a matter of serious interest.

essential prerequisite of study (b Yoma 72b). 'All
that you do, do only from love' in S Deut. 41 on xi.3.
Rabba b R. Hona said: 'A man who knows the law
but does not fear God is like a treasurer to whom have
been entrusted the keys of the interior (of the house),
but not of the exterior; how can he get in?' But all
this makes no difference to the fact that man secures
for himself righteousness and life by his study and his
fulfilment of the Torah.

IV. LAW IN THE NEW TESTAMENT

A. *Jesus and the law according to the Synoptists*

1. *The occurrence of the word*

The significance of what is denoted positively and negatively by the word νόμος in the Synoptics is by no means covered by the extent to which the actual word occurs in them. In order therefore to understand what was in fact Jesus' attitude to the law according to the Synoptists, it is necessary to refer also to certain passages in which the word νόμος is lacking.[1] In Matthew νόμος is found only eight times, in Luke nine times, in Mark it is absent altogether.

In the few passages where νόμος is found, the usage is simple. ὁ νόμος is used, except in Luke ii.23. Here νόμος has no article and appears in the phrase νόμος κυρίου which is no doubt derived from *tōrath Yahweh*.[2] Normally νόμος means the Pentateuch. When in addition the whole Scripture is to be included ὁ νόμος καὶ οἱ προφῆται is found (Matt. v.17, vii.12, xi.13, xxii.40; Luke xvi.16, xxiv.44 (expanded here by ψαλμοί). The twofold meaning of νόμος and *tōrāh* to be observed in Judaism holds good also for the synoptic use of νόμος: it means the *Law* and the *Pentateuch*, the *Scripture*. In the forefront appears its character as law, as instructions for what to do and what not to do. In Matt. xxii.36 the question ποία ἐντολὴ μεγάλη ἐν τῷ νόμῳ; does not mean which commandment in the

---

[1] Furthermore, in several passages it is doubtful whether the expression was originally part of the respective saying or statement; cf. e.g. Matt. vii.12 with Luke vi.31. A. Harnack, *Beiträge zur Einleitung in das NT*, II: *Sprüche und Reden Jesu* (1907), pp. 11 f.

[2] It is true that Luke ii.39 is different: κατὰ τὸν νόμον κυρίου.

79

Pentateuch is the greatest, but what kind of commandment is important within the whole range of the law.[1]
But here it is plain also how far from clear-cut the distinction can be. For although the Pentateuch consists
essentially of the law, the law is to be found nowhere
except in the Pentateuch. A great deal about the
relationship between the meanings of law and Pentateuch for νόμος can be learned from Matt. v.18 f.
Here Matthew places side by side: ἰῶτα ἓν ἢ μία κεραία
οὐ μὴ παρέλθῃ ἀπὸ τοῦ νόμου which suggests the notion
of Scripture, and μία τῶν ἐντολῶν τούτων τῶν ἐλαχίστων
which directs attention rather to the content expressed
in commandments.

The double expression ὁ νόμος καὶ οἱ προφῆται too
usually denotes the OT as containing commands
(Matt. v.17, vii.12, xxii.40). But in each case according
to the context it may refer to the OT with its promises
in view (Luke xxiv.44; Matt. xi.13, where, to be sure,
the inversion οἱ προφῆται καὶ ὁ νόμος is probably not
accidental). In other cases γραφή or some form of
γράφω is generally used for the OT in this sense.

It may be a matter of chance that νόμος does not
occur with its meaning extended to the whole OT,
although it is not perhaps purely fortuitous that Matt.
xii.5: οὐκ ἀνέγνωτε ἐν τῷ νομῳ; referring to Num.
xxviii.9 stands beside οὐκ ἀνέγνωτε; by itself (verse 3)
referring to I Sam. xxi.7. But νόμος is not used for the
'oral Torah', the traditional teaching, and in view of
passages like Mark vii.1 ff. this cannot be considered
an accident. The παράδοσις τῶν πρεσβύτερων in Mark
vii.5, since it is called a παράδοσις τῶν ἀνθρώπων in Mark
vii.8 cannot be recognised as having the nature of νόμος.

2. *Jesus' negation of the law*

In Jesus' preaching according to the Synoptists, His

---

[1] cf. Zahn, *Matthäus* (⁴1922), *ad loc.*

acceptance and negation of the law, censure and approval of it, stand inextricably side by side. There are no clues by which His statements may be listed according to their respective dates.[1] Hence the attempt must be made to understand these differing statements as they are found together.

Jesus rejected the essential nature and basis of the law by depriving it of its position as mediator. The relationship of man to God is no longer determined by the law and man's relationship to it. But now at the point where the nature of this relationship is determined there stands Jesus' word, in fact Jesus Himself. Man now has access to God through his relationship to Him and to the kingdom of God breaking through in Him.

Man is not finally separated from God when he transgresses the law and denies it (Matt. xxi.28 ff.). According to verse 31b the question here is not, it seems, the conflict between word and deed, but between the actual renunciation of God's law and the new experience that it is after all still possible to repent and that God's will is being done. That to transgress the law is a sin is not denied, but the point is that the hopeless situation arising out of this is brought to an end. This is the meaning of the sentence: οἱ τελῶναι καὶ αἱ πόρναι προάγουσιν ὑμᾶς εἰς τὴν βασιλείαν τοῦ θεοῦ (xxi.31b). The parables in Luke xv make this even more clear. They must be understood with xv.1 in mind. Tax collectors and sinners are with Jesus and He associated with them so far as to sit at table with them. So by this means the lost sheep and the lost coin

---

[1] cf. e.g. also Harnack, *Hat Jesus das alttestamentliche Gesetz abgeschafft?* pp. 227 ff. On the other hand H. J. Hotlzmann, *Lehrbuch der neutestamentlichen Theologie*, I (1911), pp. 202 f., attempts to establish Jesus' continuous development until He rejected legalism completely.

are found, by this means the lost son has returned home (vv. 3 ff., 8 ff., 11 ff.). Then in verses 25 ff. the contrast is shown: how the son who stayed at home derived no benefit from just staying at home. The pious son does not possess his final relationship to God, nor does the sinner attain his, through relationship to the law, neither by constantly keeping the commandments, which is not called in question, nor by openly flouting it, which is not glossed over. Only when the sinner has been admitted into the forgiving companionship of Jesus, has he found his way home to his father's house. And this fact confronts the other son, whose righteousness is based on the law, with the question whether he will rely on his obedience to the law as his hard-won prerogative, as he indicates by his complaint at the reception of his lost brother, or whether he will regard the fact that he has been preserved in obedience as permission to remain happily in his father's house. But this means that in both cases the law has been ousted from its place as mediator and that the relationship to Jesus' word and deed alone decides relationship to God.

The sayings in Matt. x.32 ff. say essentially the same. To acknowledge Jesus or to deny Him decides the eternal fate of men. Similarly the events put together in Mark ii are possible only if the law no longer plays the decisive role between God and man and thus a man is no longer justified or condemned in the sight of God according to whether his behaviour corresponds or does not correspond to the law.[1]

The pericopes about the blessing of the children in Mark x.13 ff., the beatitudes in Matt. v.3 ff. or the saying in Matt. xi.28 ff. point in the same direction. It is just to those on whom the law weighs so heavily

[1] A. Schlatter, *Markus* (1935), *ad loc.*: 'What Jesus did was based on the fact that He determined man's relationship to God not by the law, but by virtue of His mission.'

that they have no ἀνάπαυσις that this rest is brought by Jesus. The tax collector who bows himself in penitence before God and relies on God's mercy alone, receives the verdict: κατέβη οὗτος δεδικαιωμένος εἰς τὸν οἶκον αὐτοῦ παρ' ἐκεῖνον (Luke xviii.14)—rather than the man who could boast of his fulfilling of the law (cf. also Luke xvii.7 ff.). Scribes and Pharisees shut up the kingdom of heaven (Matt. xxiii.13) because they will only let those enter who fulfil the law which they control.

Moreover, this basically different position of the law occurs also in such sentences and contexts as those where the dawn of the new age is regarded as the essence of the new order of things. This supplements what has been established so far and guards it against misunderstanding, by pointing out that there is no question of disclosing what had always been present, of clearing up a pernicious error, but that a new act of God is involved, which had existed only as a promise and had not yet been carried out.[1] Ὁ νόμος καὶ οἱ προφῆται μέχρι Ἰωάννου· ἀπὸ τότε ἡ βασιλεία τοῦ θεοῦ εὐαγγελίζεται (Luke xvi.16; cf. Matt. xv.13). Luke is not likely to have imported an impossible meaning into this sentence by placing before it the saying against those who justify themselves before men, but of whose hearts God knows ὅτι τὸ ἐν ἀνθρώποις ὑψηλὸν βδέλυγμα ἐνώπιον τοῦ θεοῦ (Luke xvi.15) and by stating in the sentence following after it that the law retains its significance and does not lose its validity by being

---

[1] B. Weiss, *Lehrbuch der biblischen Theologie des NT* (⁷1903), p. 82, probably means something similar when he distinguishes Jesus' new understanding of the law from older thought by saying that in it 'the standard of God's perfect will . . . had not yet everywhere found adequate expression corresponding to the perfected state of the theocracy or the kingdom of God'. Jesus interprets the meaning of the law having in mind the complete revelation of God which has appeared in Him, *op. cit.*, p. 86.

violated (verse 17 f.). Thus, now that the dawn of God's kingdom is being announced, the criterion which God applies is no longer the law and the works of the law achieved by man by himself (cf. the similies of the old garment and of the wineskins in Mark ii.21 f.).[1]

But this changed situation and age are wholly tied to the word and person of Him who brings the change about. Mark ii.21 demonstrates this by using as the occasion for these sayings the antithesis between Jesus' disciples and those of John. Because the disciples belong to Jesus, they belong to the new age. This means that the Synoptists interpret this freedom from the law with Jesus as fundamentally messianic, christological (cf. Luke ii.41 ff.). So Matt. xvii.24 ff.: as the son Jesus is free from the law, even though He nevertheless observes it.

Jesus bases man's relationship to God on his relationship to Himself and to the kingdom of God which He is bringing in. Thus as the dispenser of forgiveness He addresses a call in particular to sinners. By these acts He definitely negates the law which stands as a mediator between God and man, and thereby rejects the righteousness derived from the law. It is by means of the person of Jesus Himself that the law has been expelled from its key position.

3. *Jesus' acceptance of the law*

This new position and the rejection of the law arising out of it alone make it possible to understand correctly Jesus' acceptance of the law. For it is obvious that by ousting the law from its place as mediator, there is no intention of rejecting it altogether.

(*a*) Jesus recognises the law by behaving as the dispenser of forgiveness when for example He calls the

[1] Rengstorf, *Lucas* (NT Deutsch) *ad loc.*; Wellhausen, *Markus*, *ad loc.*

tax collectors and sinners to join His company (Luke xv). On these occasions the opinion is quite openly expressed that He is dealing with the sick (Mark ii.17), with the lost, with those about to die (Luke xv.3 ff., 24, 32). Thus by the verdict to which His forgiveness is attached, Jesus gives the law particular prominence.

The law is right in demanding obedience, since to refuse it means death. Therefore a doctrine which enlightens the merely alleged sinner cannot create a new situation. This can be done only by the eschatological act of forgiveness, i.e. an act which bears witness to God's kingdom. Consequently it is not a new doctrine about God and His will, a new religion, which fashions the new relationship to God. It is the dawn of the age of salvation, and therefore the act of forgiveness. Hence not only is the law driven out from its position as mediator, but the verdict of the law and thus its claim are at the same time recognised as just, and indeed it is presupposed as necessary.[1]

(b) Moreover, all the pericopes cited show that Jesus does not wish to eliminate obedience, even though He does not base the relationship to God upon it (cf. Matt. xxi.28 ff.). When the lost son decides to go back home, it means that he is ready to return to his obedience (Luke xv.19; cf. also Luke xix.1 ff.). When Jesus delivers a man from the weight of the law's yoke, He calls him to take up His yoke (Matt. xi.29). The righteousness of the disciples must exceed that of the scribes and Pharisees, not in the subtlety of their legal casuistry, but in their whole-hearted devotion to the will of God (Matt. v.20). By bringing in the βασιλεία τοῦ θεοῦ, Jesus proclaims and produces true obedience and thereby recognises the law in such a manner as to

---

[1] A. Schlatter, *Geschichte des Christus* (²1923), p. 174, says that Jesus' 'ethical propositions are not meditations on problems of ethics, but parts of His call to repentance'.

G

lead to its fulfilment. The good tree bears good fruit (Matt. vii.16 ff.). This simile does not represent the relationship between deed and intention, but that between these two on the one hand and on the other the status of child of God reached through Jesus. If this makes the tree good, then the good fruit must come.

(*c*) So it is not surprising that according to the account of the Synoptists Jesus Himself keeps the law. For instance He wears as a matter of course the garments prescribed by the law (Matt. ix.20 f., xiv.36).[1] In Luke's story of the childhood, he takes a serious interest in the fact that Jesus was placed under the law; and indeed He receives the prophetic witness just because He is being placed under the law (Luke ii.24-25, 27-28).[2] But there is something more: the goal of the messianic activity will not be reached *until all is accomplished* (Matt. v.18)[3] The coming of Jesus is just what is meant by the fulfilment[4] of the law, and the cross is understood as the union of the consummated obedience to the will of God declared in the scriptures with love towards the brethren in the act of self-offering. It is true that the Synoptists did not explicitly state that in this they saw Jesus fulfilling the law, but their presentation suggests it (cf. also Matt. iii.15).[5]

(*d*) As, according to this, Jesus acknowledges that the law represents God's good purpose for Himself, so

---

[1] Branscomb, pp. 115 f.———[2] Zahn, *Lucas* (^{3},^{4}1920), *ad loc.*

[3] Schlatter, *Matthäus, ad loc.*

[4] According to verse 19 πληροῦν is not to be understood as 'making perfect' in regard to its content, but in the sense of 'putting it into effect'. Contrary to A. Harnack, 'Geschichte eines programmatischen Wortes Jesu (Matt. v.17) in der ältesten Kirche', *Sitzungsbericht der Preussischen (Deutschen) Akademie . . . zu Berlin* (phil.-hist. Klasse) (1913), pp. 184 ff.

[5] cf. Schlatter, *Matthäus* on v.18.

it does also for others. When questioned about right action Jesus replies: τὰς ἐντολὰς οἶδας (Mark x.19). He recognises that no other purpose is good than that of God revealed in the law.[1] Beyond this there is no other goodness represented by Him (Mark x.18, similarly Luke x.25 ff.).

Jesus accepts the law because it requires obedience in action and is not content with a disposition which cannot be checked. He rejects those who confess Him as Lord whilst at the same time doing ἀνομία[2] (Matt. vii.23). The law is concerned with doing; it is not enough merely to know God's good purpose (Luke x.28).

In concrete terms the law demands self-denying love of God and of one's neighbour[3] (Mark xii.28 and parallels); the addition in Matt. xxii.40 is to the point. This unvarying summing up in the law of love is expressed in other passages also. Thus for example in Matt. vii.12 or Matt. xxiv.12: διὰ τὸ πληθυνθῆναι τὴν ἀνομίαν ψυγήσεται ἡ ἀγάπη τῶν πολλῶν. Lawlessness and lovelessness correspond to one another (cf. also Matt. v.43 ff.).

Thus there exists also a direct positive connexion between the law and Jesus as the Christ, in so far as genuine obedience to the law is fulfilled by following Christ. The rich man would bring his fulfilment of the law to completion by the utter surrender of himself in following Jesus (Mark x.17 ff.). When in Mark xii.34 the questioner acknowledges the law's radical demand for love, he is not far from the kingdom of God, but he does not yet belong to it, in so far as he still expects his observance of the law to be his own achievement.[4]

---

[1] P. Feine, *Theologie des NT* (⁴1922), pp. 24 ff.
[2] cf. on this word, below, pp. 135ff.
[3] cf. also Harnack, p. 229.
[4] cf. Schniewind, *Markus* (NT Deutsch, 1952), *ad loc*.

(e) Side by side with this definite affirmation of the law there stands Jesus' censure of it. But it is a censure which actually serves to affirm and support it, not to bring it to an end. Jesus criticises the law *firstly* in so far as it protects man's disobedience against God's demands. He does not accept as perfect obedience a man's observance of the law's individual precepts, if he is not also ready for complete surrender (Mark x.21 and parallels). Even the fourth commandment is set aside by Jesus if it is brought forward as a hindrance to hearing Jesus' call to follow Him (Matt. viii.21 f.; cf. also Luke xii.52 f.). Similarly if the law is observed primarily for the sake of being recognised by men, Jesus did not recognise this observance at all (Matt. xxiii.5 ff., vi.1 ff.). Thus Jesus did not, for example, reject only the appeal to the 'tradition of the elders' in face of the plain duty of the law (ἀφέντες τὴν ἐντολὴν τοῦ θεοῦ κρατεῖτε τὴν παράδοσιν τῶν ἀνθρώπων Mark vii.8 ff.), but also the appeal to what is demanded by the letter of the law in face of the absolute claim of God, as well as of the claim of one's neighbour.

This is the meaning, for example, of the pericope concerning the sabbath in Mark iii.1 ff. When the question concerning good and evil is raised, i.e. in this case the question concerning the will of God as revealed in that actual moment by the neighbour's need for help, then the question of what is permitted or prohibited by the commandment about the sabbath is solved as well. Certainly God's will appears in the law, but it is not tied to the law to such an extent that by an appeal to it God's will concerning the obligation to one's neighbour can thereby be evaded.

Thus it is not a case of reducing the law to a system of morality, but of exposing its basic principles by raising the question concerning actual obedience in loving one's neighbour.

This removal of all limits to the duty of obedience is assisted by tracing the law back to the love of God and of one's neighbour. As contrasted with similar examples in Judaism, this summary does not spring from a concern for a systematic clarification of the multifarious precepts of the law, nor does it derive from a kind of playful edifying tendency, nor does it aim at relaxing the law and making God's will innocuous. On the contrary, its purpose is to expose the law's basic principle,[1] to admit nothing as fulfilling the law which is not at its heart obedience to God and service to one's neighbour. Above all its object is to prevent obedience and service being refused by appealing to the observance of the commandments. At the same time the rabbinic distinction between a legal obligation and a voluntary act of love disappears (cf. Matt. iii.15; Luke x.28 ff.; Mark x.17 ff.).[2]

The censure on the law implicit in thus unifying it, is therefore an affirmation of it in a fundamental sense, and means bringing it back to its original OT meaning, namely that God has a claim on man and uses this claim to direct his attention to his neighbour. Thus, in the manner in which the prophets understood the law, a way is made through the law to reach God Himself and His will is to be recognised both within the actual law and outside it. There is this difference between Jesus and the prophets, that they only promise the act of God which produces this obedience, whilst Jesus himself offers and in fact is this act.

Therefore when Jesus rejects casuistry, it is not to be thought that He wishes to make the OT commandments more humane, or rational or moral,[3] nor to

---

[1] R. Bultmann, 'Jesus und Paulus', in: *Jesus Christus im Zeugnis der heiligen Schrift und der Kirche* (1936), pp. 74 ff.

[2] Bultmann, *Die Bedeutung* . . ., pp. 193 f.

[3] Certanly Jesus makes the position of men before the law clear

release them from the nationalistic restrictions into a broad universalism.[1] But Jesus' first desire is to attach serious importance to God's holiness which claims the whole man, as contrasted with the protection which man seeks in the law from the sheer absoluteness of this claim. This is made particularly clear in Matt. xxiii.23 where Jesus is not objecting in any way to keeping the small precepts of the law, but condemns severely the idea that one can thereby feel free to neglect the observance of the βαρύτερα τοῦ νόμου.

Secondly, this is closely connected with the fact that Jesus criticises the law in so far as it does not lay bare the root of sin, since, although it condemns the deed, it does not condemn the condition of the heart and mind which causes the deed.

Thirdly and lastly, this is the place to speak of the censure of the law which arises from the fact that the law as it is assumes the sin of man to be an accepted, unalterable state of affairs. Mark x.5: πρὸς τὴν σκληροκαρδίαν ὑμῶν ἔγραψεν (sc. Moses) ὑμῖν τὴν ἐντολὴν ταύτην. Belonging to Jesus and to the βασιλεία τοῦ θεοῦ marks the restoring of order in accordance with creation, an order which does not presuppose sin as an accepted unalterable state of affairs.[2] This is part

especially by means of ethical precepts, not by cultic or ritual ones. But in any case the essential point which He wishes to make with regard to the law does not consist in placing the former on principle above the latter, even if there can be any question of such a thing. Even in Mark vii the alternatives are not primarily concerned with an 'ethical' or a 'ritual' understanding of the law, but with real obedience or the concealing of disobedience by an appeal to the law. Cf. also F. Büchsel, *Theol. des NT* (1935), pp. 22 f. For another view cf., for example, H. Weinel, *Biblische Theologie des NT* (1928), pp. 82 ff.

[1] Weinel, pp. 85 ff. lays stress on this and so does Herkenrath p. 132.

[2] The treatment of this particular question shows how freedom is not excluded by a direct referring of the commandments to

of the meaning in the antitheses in Matt. v.21 ff., particularly clear perhaps in verse 38 ff. The law curbs the unrestrained thirst for vengeance; Jesus frees His own completely from it. In so far as the law presupposes the sin of man, it is annulled by Jesus, because He creates the obedience of love which gives up all claims to itself and its rights, and relies on God alone.

In this way the law is established all the more firmly. But at the same time it is completely clear that the law in Jesus' new conception of it is no longer understood as something to be fulfilled by man with the idea that thereby he wins for himself God's verdict vindicating him. On the contrary, the fulfilling of the claim presupposes his status of a child of God,[1] a status which comes into existence through companionship with Jesus and has its being in the forgiveness thus bestowed.

4. *The relationship between the negation and the acceptance of the law*

It is thus evident that the recognition of the law by affirming and censuring it has two main aspects. It is a call for total repentance to which the demands of the law give depth and reality, and it shows the nature of genuine obedience, of the new righteousness. Neither of these can be dissociated from the fact that Jesus does not base the relationship between man and God on the observance of the law, but establishes it on God's new creative act of forgiveness. On the one hand a way has been opened up through the law to God's direct claim and it is recognised that its quite new interpretation involves condemnation; on the other hand man has been set free from the mediation of the law

God. Because marriage is divinely ordained, it is completely binding for those who are bound to God. But for this very reason there may be release from this order for the sake of the kingdom of God.   [1] cf. Büchsel, p. 26.

and its observance. These two sets of circumstances challenge and condition each other.[1] It is only when a man renounces his own achievements and accepts forgiveness that he becomes capable of really facing the judgement of the law and of offering the obedience of love. But at the same time the thorough establishment of its claim and of its verdict raises the question concerning God's new act for man and for the world.

B.   *The conflict concerning the law*

1. *The primitive community*

The sources provide no reliable picture as to how the primitive community understood the law during the earliest period. It is no doubt true that the community did in fact observe the law. But in what sense it did so cannot be gathered unequivocally from the account in the Acts of the Apostles, since we must note its tendency to obliterate differences in this matter.[2] Theological reflexion was likely in its beginnings to have been concerned much less with the law than with understanding Jesus as the Messiah promised by the scripture.[3] The problem of the law made its appearance as a subject requiring attention only when the community began to spread to former Gentiles or into Gentile spheres generally.[4] The first place where we can get a clear indication of the points of view regarding

---

[1] The contrary holds good in Judaism. The position of the law as mediator is maintained and the attempt is made to be vindicated in God's sight by one's own efforts, and this attitude cannot be dissociated from the secret refusal of obedience with the help of the law and from renouncing complete penitence.

[2] O. Weizsäcker, *Das apostolische Zeitalter der christlichen Kirche* (1902), pp. 169 ff., ET of 2nd ed. 2 vols, (1894/5), I pp. 200 ff.

[3] cf. P. Wernle, *Die Anfänge unserer Religion* ([2]1904), p. 108.

[4] The problem of winning the Samaritans (Acts viii) was not quite so difficult, yet similar in some respects.

this problem occurs at the 'Apostolic Council'. Acts xv and Galatians ii agree to a large extent in their account of it.[1] The basic understanding of the law by the primitive community can be most readily deduced from the decisions taken on that occasion.

(a) The situation at the Apostolic Council, according in the main to Galatians, is as follows: firstly, the agreement of the gospel preached by Paul with that of the primitive community was confirmed. Such agreement was not brought about for the first time on this occasion. (Cf. Gal. ii.2: ἀνεθέμην αὐτοῖς τὸ εὐαγγέλιον ὃ κησύσσω ἐν τοῖς ἔθνεσιν, and verse 6: ἐμοὶ οἱ δοκοῦντες οὐδὲν προσανέθεντο).

Since from the outset the problem at issue concerned the law, it is impossible to assume that this agreement did not apply also to the basic problem of the attitude to the law. If it did so, then the agreement on the separation of the εὐαγγέλιον τῆς ἀκροβυστίας and the εὐαγγέλιον τῆς περιτομῆς (Gal. ii.7) does not mean that Paul recognised a ἕτερον εὐαγγέλιον (Gal. i.6). This is corroborated by Gal. ii.16: εἰδότες δὲ οὐ δικαιοῦται ἄνθρωπος ἐξ ἔργων νόμου . . . , καὶ ἡμεῖς εἰς Χριστὸν Ἰησοῦν ἐπιστεύσαμεν, ἵνα δικαιωθῶμεν ἐκ πίστεως Χριστοῦ καὶ οὐκ ἐξ ἔργων νόμου.[2] Whether or not the verses in Gal. ii.15 ff. are to be considered as addressed to Peter makes no difference to the fact that Paul takes Peter's assent to this statement for granted and assumes it to be well known. The dispute concerns the practical conclusions to be drawn from this common basic point of view. Acts xv for its part confirms this formulation of the problem and this agreed answer. Those who came from Judaea to Antioch taught the brethren ὅτι ἐὰν μὴ περιτμηθῆτε τῷ ἔθει τῷ

[1] There are too many objections to the thesis of Weizsäcker that Acts xv was written with Galatians ii in mind.

[2] cf. Weizsäcker, p. 160, ET I, pp. 190 f.

Μωυσέως, οὐ δύνασθε σωθῆναι (Acts xv.1; cf. xv. 5). And Acts xv.11 gives the reply: ἀλλὰ διὰ τῆς χάριτος τοῦ κυρίου Ἰησοῦ πιστεύομεν σωθῆναι καθ' ὃν τρόπον κἀκεῖνοι. Although it is obviously most improbable that this report contains Peter's own words, yet it is equally obvious that a definite conclusion follows from Acts xv in its agreement with Gal. ii, namely that there was unanimity in a negative sense as regards the question whether the law was necessary for salvation, since for both parties the σωτηρία, the δικαιοῦσθαι, was through faith in the Lord Jesus alone.

Secondly, it is just as certain that the practical problems extending beyond this fundamental unanimity had however not been settled so far as to render impossible the dispute in Antioch described by Paul in Gal. ii.1 ff.

In order to understand this passage it must be noted that Paul has no word of blame, either directly or indirectly, for those coming on behalf of James (cf. the distinction made in Gal. ii.4: παρείσαπτοι ψευδάδελφοι).[1] The practical question is, whether and how far Jews by birth may live together in one community with Gentile Christians who do not keep the law, and in particular may have fellowship with them at table and at the celebration of the Lord's supper,[2] since in that case they would have to sacrifice essential parts of the strict observance of the law. So a clear position was reached for purely Gentile-Christian and for purely Jewish-Christian communities to the extent that the former with the assent of the primitive community were free from the law and the latter with Paul's assent kept the law.[3]

---

[1] cf. Kittel, pp. 145 ff., 152.

[2] According to Kittel, p. 149, n. 1, it is not certain that fellowship at the celebration of the Lord's supper was in dispute.

[3] Schlatter, *Geschichte der ersten Christenheit*, pp. 70, 150 ff.,

The outcome of the Apostolic Council is thus as follows: The law is not to be kept with the idea that its observance procures justification. Salvation is secured for Gentiles and for Jews by faith in Jesus; but nevertheless the law remains obligatory for Jews. For this reason it seems to have been recognised as necessary and appropriate by Paul and the primitive community alike that the preaching of the gospel to the Gentiles and to the Jews should be kept separate (Gal. ii.7).

(b) Now this raises the question as to the reason for which the obligation on Jewish Christians to keep the law was maintained. This matter can be judged by considering whether Paul could give his consent to the argument. The circumstances of the conflict made it necessary that the reasons should be considered at this point. Up till then the situation had been taken for granted without there being any need to think out particular grounds for it.

The main reason is a concern for the possibility of a mission to the Jews. For to preach Jesus as the Christ of the scripture was no longer acceptable for Jews if his adherents abandoned God's law. In that case this community would in their eyes have been condemned from the outset.[1] I Cor. ix.20 f. proves quite clearly that Paul could agree to this point of view. He himself behaved τοῖς ὑπὸ νόμον ὡς ὑπὸ νόμον, μὴ ὢν αὐτὸς ὑπὸ νόμον in order that he might win those under the law. He neither demands nor demonstrates his freedom from the law by transgressing the law.

Naturally the practical questions in the mixed com-

J. Weiss, *Das Urchristentum* (1917), p. 205; Weizsäcker, pp. 164 ff.. ET I, pp. 196 ff. A different view in Meyer, *Ursprung*, III, pp. 424 ff.

[1] cf. J. Weiss, p. 198; Schlatter, *Geschichte der ersten Christenheit*, 14.

munities were bound to become difficult. If we are to understand these matters, we must see the decisive part played by the Apostolic Decree (Acts xv.23 ff., xxi.25), which is certainly not an invention of Acts.[1] On the contrary the only question which arises is whether it is part of the Apostolic Council or is the outcome of the subsequent incident in Antioch. In no case is the decree to be understood as the lowest ethical standard, as an extract from the law by way of a compromise to make at least its fundamental basis compulsory in place of the whole law.[2] That is ruled out by the choice of the conditions as well as by the general Jewish understanding of the law; it would also have made Paul's assent impossible. Nor does the chief object in view seem to be to guard against 'libertine' Gnostic ideas; for in that case the third and fourth points would remain unintelligible, and moreover it is hardly possible to think that no reason for such action should have been given. On the contrary there are no general grounds at all for distrusting the motive given in Acts xv.21: Μωυσῆς γὰρ ἐκ γενεῶν ἀρχάιων κατὰ πόλιν τοὺς κηρύσσοντας αὐτὸν ἔχει ἐν ταῖς συναγωγαῖς κατὰ πᾶν σάββατον ἀναγινωσκόμενος. Now since in the Jewish synagogues of the Diaspora fellowship at the divine service with the uncircumcised took place, such a fellowship between Gentiles and Jews in the Christian community could be justified to Jewry, if the rules laid down in the decree were accepted by Gentile Christians. This did not mean that the obligation to keep the law was restricted to these matters for Jewish Christians. But they could enter into fellowship with those Gentiles who accepted these rules, without offending the Jews.[3]

(c) From the way the primitive community made its

---

[1] Weizsäcker, pp. 175 ff., ET, I, pp. 208 ff.
[2] cf. Schlatter, *Geschichte der ersten Christenheit*, pp. 158 f.
[3] cf. J. Weiss, p. 237; Weizsäcker, p. 180, ET I p. 214.

decisions in these cases on principle and in practice, it is possible to deduce its view of the law even during the earlier period. The fact that it was bound by the law was not legalism in the sense that observance of the law was a prerequisite for membership of the Messianic kingdom. But it considered this obligation as the obedience demanded of it practically as a result of its membership, an obedience also to be rendered by it in the service of the gospel for the sake of love. But what held the community together and kept it apart from the rest was not a particular understanding of the law, but faith in Jesus as Lord and Christ.

Now whence comes this peculiar attitude to the law, being at the same time both free from it and bound by it? The presentation in the Synoptic gospels tells us that this attitude to the law is derived from Jesus.[1] And indeed the agreement between Jesus' attitude to the law as portrayed by the Synoptists and that of the primitive community is in fact so striking that there must be a direct connexion between them. The only question to be asked is whether that picture of Jesus' attitude to the law does not owe its existence to the understanding of the law in the primitive community.

But in this last case only two sources of this attitude call for consideration. Either it was deduced from the confession of Jesus as Lord by reasoning and was demanded by the historical events; the primitive community would then have had to understand it as revelation and guidance from their Lord present with them in the Holy Spirit. Or on the other hand there were amongst them influences from Hellenistic Jewry which toned down in various ways the strictly Jewish point of view towards the law. The story of Cornelius (Acts x f., cf. Acts xv.7 ff.!), for example, seems to be an argument for the first possibility; for the second the

[1] cf. Weizsäcker, pp. 625 f., ET, II pp. 341 ff.

events concerning Stephen (Acts vi f.). But on closer examination this latter possibility drops out. For in that case Stephen with his conception of the law could not have met with opposition from the Hellenistic-Jewish synagogue in particular (Acts vi.9 ff.). Moreover in essentials, in attitude and motive, none of the Hellenistic-Jewish conceptions of the law approximated in the least to the primitive Christian one. It is perhaps going too far to expect from this direction even a greater readiness and openness towards that aspect of Jesus' message which proclaimed freedom from the law.[1] Stephen was condemned for his Christian, not his Hellenistic, attitude to the law.

As regards the first of the possibilities mentioned, it must at any rate be observed that the Jewish theology of the Messiah and the ideas attached to it concerning the relationship of the Messiah to the law, would not have assisted the primitive Christian attitude to develop out of the confession of Jesus as Lord, but on the contrary would have hindered it.[2] Besides in view of the nature of the tradition almost insuperable difficulties would arise on just this question, if the synoptic presentation were derived from the primitive Christian attitude.

Thus it is most likely, speaking historically, that the Synoptists' accounts concerning Jesus' attitude to the law are on the whole true to history, and that therefore the primitive community owed its attitude to the law fundamentally to that of Jesus.[3]

[1] For this question cf. J. Weiss, pp. 121 ff., 198; M. Meyer, *Ursprung*, III, pp. 271 ff.; Weizsäcker, pp. 52 ff., ET, I pp. 63 ff.; M. Maurenbrecher, *Von Jerusalem nach Rom* (1910), pp. 113, 114 f., 115.   [2] cf. p. 74.

[3] This does not make such a story as that about Cornelius unnecessary, since it was not left to the community to decide when freedom from the law became for it actually necessary and right.

(d) The struggles, motives and decisions which emerged into daylight at the Apostolic Council and from the resultant events enable the further development within the primitive community to be understood as well. The extreme party, customarily called Judaisers, maintains in spite of the Apostolic Council that circumcision and the law must be imposed on Gentile Christians too, since otherwise they could not attain to salvation, to the community of Christ.[1] They disseminate this idea zealously, especially in the Pauline communities. Nevertheless it remains an open question whether the circumstances presupposed in Romans are likewise to be explained by Judaistic propaganda.[2]

Their motives are, according to Galatians, fear of persecution for the sake of the cross, coupled with lust for personal power (Gal. vi.12 f.). Behind this there might be the change in the missionary attitude of the primitive community which desired to avoid all unpleasantness from Jewry, even to the extent of renouncing the gospel of justification by faith in Jesus alone.[3] It must be assumed that there were also morally less unworthy motives for the attitude of the Judaisers. For to some of those who had grown up in the law the idea that through faith in Jesus the law could, or indeed must, be renounced, would have seemed quite simply impossible.

The considerations advanced by the Judaisers in support of their teaching were apparently firstly a reference to the commands of the scriptures, as the polemic in Galatians iii f. shows, next a reference to the practice of the primitive community, even no doubt

[1] Weizsäcker, pp. 216 ff., ET, I pp. 257 ff.; Schlatter, *Geschichte der ersten Christenheit*, p. 152.

[2] cf. Weizsäcker, pp. 424 ff., ET, II pp. 99 ff.

[3] There may have been associated with this the idea that only in this way could the advantages be preserved for Christendom which the protection of the Roman Empire involved for Jewry.

to that of Jesus Himself. This was combined with dis-
crediting Paul's apostolate, as may be seen for example
in II Cor. xi; I Cor. i.12; Gal. i. A reference to the
ethical results, believed necessarily to follow from the
Pauline doctrine of the law, will have contributed in
part, and indeed no doubt particularly in the more
important cases. This may even have been the chief
motive. Yet this seems to be presupposed in Romans
more than in Galatians.[1] In these matters it is in itself
not probable that there was behind this activity a
homogeneous theological reasoning, likely to be the
same everywhere, since the first consideration for these
people seems to have been not the reasoning, but
interest in the law itself.

A later continuation of this trend which was bound
to lose ground in the course of time with the historical
changes which took place, is found in the group of the
Ebionites who then separated from the church. They
upheld the binding force of the law on all Christians.[2]
Perhaps they are to be distinguished from the Nazar-
enes[3] who only clung to the law for themselves, but
released the Gentile Christians from it and recognised
Paul.

(e) The attitude of James and Peter and of the
community who followed their lead must be kept
separate from this Judaising trend. They seem in the
main to have kept to the line adopted by the Apostolic
Council. At any rate this corresponds to the picture
of James given in Acts xxi.18 ff. and is confirmed in
Josephus' account of James' death.[4] As regards Peter,
it is easiest to assume that he returned to the line taken
by the Apostolic Council and by James after he had for
a time in Antioch conformed to Paul's point of view.

---

[1] Weizsäcker, p. 428, ET, II p. 104.
[2] J. Weiss, p. 572.   [3] J. Weiss, p. 523.
[4] Jos. *Ant.* 20.200. On this J. Weiss, p. 552, n. 2; Kittel, p. 146.

At any rate the attempt to make Peter the champion
of the Judaisers[1] is not sufficiently substantiated in the
extant sources. Besides, it is in itself improbable.

Thus the authoritative circles of primitive Christianity understood the law as follows: they regarded it as
the standard for the obedience owed by Jewish Christians, and furthermore knew that they were committed
to it with a view to winning Jewry for the gospel. But
they did not regard the observance of it as the means
whereby man is justified in the sight of God. In consequence they held brotherly intercourse with Gentile
Christians, even if the latter did not keep the law. In
mixed communities, the Gentile Christians were expected to observe such rules as made intercourse with
them on the part of Jewish Christians appear defensible
to the Jewish community.

2. *Pauline usage*

The Pauline usage of νόμος is not quite uniform, since
Paul uses νόμος also in some cases in which he is not denoting the OT law. But nevertheless the starting point
is not a general meaning of νόμος, at times to be used
chiefly for the Mosaic law.[2] It is in fact the traditional
use of the word for the Israelite law in particular. Hence
also what νόμος signifies is assumed to be self-evident
and so usually no more precise designation is added.[3]

---

[1] Especially Meyer, *Ursprung und Anfänge des Christentums*, III,
pp. 434 ff. For Romans, cf. H. Lietzmann, *Sitzungsbericht der
preussischen (deutschen) Akademie . . . Berlin* (1930), and E. Hirsch,
ZNW 29 (1930), pp. 63 ff., for a criticism of this.

[2] Cremer *Biblisch-Theologisch.Wörterbuch*, ed. Kögel ([11]1923),
(ET of ed. 2, 2 vols. 1878-86) endeavours to distinguish between
the term νόμος in general and its definite application to Israel's
divine law. Yet he says himself that in the case of Paul too the use
of the term is qualified by what he says about the Israelite law.

[3] I Cor. ix.9: ὁ Μωυσέως νόμος; Rom. vii.22, 25, viii.7: ὁ νόμος
τοῦ θεοῦ (the context makes it necessary to add τοῦ θεοῦ for emphasis).

H

In accordance with rabbinic usage, that which νόμος is intended to convey can be exemplified by the Decalogue, which is thus, as it were, specifically 'the law' (Rom. xiii.8 ff., ii.20 ff., vii.7). Yet Paul makes no distinction on principle between the Decalogue and the rest of the legal material. With an appropriate noun in the genitive νόμος can also be employed for a particular individual law, thus Rom. vii.2: νόμος τοῦ ἀνδρός, meaning no doubt in the first place the law in force in respect of the husband,[1] signifying here the law binding the wife to the husband, not something like the law issuing from the husband.

νόμος is regarded by Paul chiefly as that which demands action by man, namely as a definite purpose. Hence the law is 'kept' (Rom. ii.25; cf. Gal. v.3, vi.13). Hence there are ἔργα νόμου required by the law, works to be performed in conformity with the law (Rom. iii.28 et passim). This alone makes sense, for example, of the question in Rom. vii.7: ὁ νόμος ἁμαρτία; which means: is the purpose of the law sinful? The positive aspect of this is in Rom. vii.12: ὁ νόμος ἅγιος. The purpose of the law, the requirement, of the law, is holy.[2]

But even if the emphasis in νόμος thus lies on its nature as God's demand, it is just in the Mosaic law of the OT that this can be grasped.[3] The shift of

---

[1] cf. for example Lev. vi.18 (EVV 25) = the law in force in respect of the sin offering.

[2] Schlatter, *Gottes Gerechtigkeit. Ein Kommentar zum Römerbrief* (³1959), on Rom. vii.7.

[3] cf. A. W. Slaten, 'The Qualitative Use of νόμος in the Pauline Epistles', *American Journal of Theology*, 23 (1919), pp. 213 ff. Even if Paul often uses νόμος qualitatively, 'that is with especial emphasis upon the essential law-quality of law, its "lawness", so to speak' (214), its specific relationship to the OT law is not thereby disclaimed (217 n. 1). But ὁ νόμος with the article, as in Rom. iv.15, has this qualitative meaning no less than νόμος without the article in Rom. iv.14.

emphasis, the value set by Paul on the nature of the law as being the living purpose of God, as contrasted with the value set by the rabbis on the declaration of this purpose once for all, is not accidental, although their usage agrees on the whole. Yet we must not confuse with this the question whether or not a difference does exist between the use of νόμος with or without the article.[1] At any rate we do not find that νόμος means 'a' law whilst ὁ νόμος means 'the' law.

This fact should be noted in the exegesis for example of Rom. ii.12 ff. Ὅσοι ἐν νόμῳ ἥμαρτον are not such people who have sinned owing to the existence of some law or other, but, as contrasted with those who ἀνόμως ἥμαρτον (verse 12a), they are those who knew the one divine law and yet sinned. The Gentiles in Rom. ii.14: νόμον μὴ ἔχοντες do not know the particular OT law. Within Paul's range of thought there was probably no nation which had no law of some sort, and even a law with religious sanction. If these Gentiles do by nature, i.e. without knowing the revealed law, the things that it commands, this makes them ἑαυτοῖς νόμος, not 'a' law, but 'the' law to themselves.[2] If νόμος without the article implied here a generalisation of the concept of law, the train of thought would be broken.

Not every nation's moral or political and social code is considered by Paul to have the nature of the νόμος.[3]

---

[1] cf. for this E. Grafe, *Die Paulinische Lehre vom Gesetz* ([2]1893), pp. 3 ff.; there the earlier literature on the question is also to be found. P. Feine, *Die Theologie des NT* ([4]1922), p. 218. Blass-Debrunner, *Grammatik* (ed. 6) § 258, 2. (An English translation of the Blass-Debrunner *Greek Grammar of the New Testament and other early Christian Literature* is shortly to be published by the Cambridge University Press and the University of Chicago Press).

[2] Schlatter, *op. cit.* (p. 102, n. 2), *ad loc.*

[3] Rom. v.14 is typical. Here the term νόμος is not used in the case of Adam, although since he had transgressed a definite command it was a matter of παράβασις of the same kind as took

Hence he does not use νόμος in the plural, not even in the manner of Hellenistic Judaism where οἱ νόμοι are used for the OT law; still less does he place similar laws of other nations beside the OT law.[1] The law is one, the revealed purpose of the one God.

Its central meaning as God's demand is also expressed by the fact that νόμος is referred to as if it were a personal power. In Rom. iii.19 the law speaks; in Rom. iv.15 it produces; in Rom. vii.1 it is binding; in I Cor. ix.8 it says. Occasionally νόμος might actually be rendered as God, in so far as He reveals Himself in the law. But this does not in any way suggest that the law is being made into some kind of hypostasis, for beside these expressions there always stand corresponding ones of an impersonal nature (Rom. iii.20, iv.15, vii.2; I Cor. ix.9.

In addition to this principal use of νόμος, the other important meaning of the rabbinic tōrāh also occurs, namely νόμος = Pentateuch, without regard to its nature as demand.[2] In Gal. iv.21 νόμος is obviously used intentionally in a twofold sense: λέγετέ μοι οἱ ὑπὸ νόμον θέλοντες εἶναι, τὸν νόμον οὐκ ἀκούετε; The second time νόμος means simply the narrative in the Pentateuch. Hence in Rom. iii.21 beside this νόμος are placed the prophets; together they mean the whole scripture. In his proofs from scripture, Paul likes to put a passage from the Torah beside one from the prophets.[3] But this does not prevent him from using

place later under the law. So here too it is not a question of an extension of νόμος in the direction of a general concept of law.

[1] cf. Brandt, pp. 8 f.; Lohmeyer, p. 14.

[2] It is true that in such cases occasionally a saying from scripture itself, containing no command, and the moral to be drawn from it, are used to inculcate again right action; yet law is here not understood directly as demand (e.g. I Cor. xiv.21).

[3] e.g. Rom. ix.12, x.6 ff., 13, 19 ff., vi.10 ff.; II Cor. vi.16 ff.; Gal. iv.27, 30. Cf. the list in Michel pp. 12 f., 53. For the rabbinic

νόμος for the whole of the OT as well. In I Cor. xiv.21
a passage from the prophets is cited with the words ἐν
τῷ νόμῳ γέγραπται.[1] Similarly Rom. iii.19 sums up
passages from all the parts of scripture in the phrase
ὅσα ὁ νόμος λέγει.

Finally Paul employs νόμος also in a figurative sense.
Usually it appears in that case with an appropriate
noun in the genitive or some other word of explanation.
In Rom. iii.17 νόμος πίστεως is contrasted with νόμος
ἔργων. Thus νόμος has here the wider meaning of a
divine ordinance which describes faith, not works, as
the right behaviour of men; hence any boasting before
God becomes impossible. Just as νόμος ἔργων can be
understood as the law which results in works, so can
νόμος πίστεως as God's ordinance demanding faith. In
Rom. vii.21 the best meaning will be obtained by
taking νόμος in a figurative sense.[2] The meaning of
νόμος would then be the fact that evil is close at hand
when I want to do right. This rule would then be
called 'law' because there is no escape from its validity.
In addition, νόμος is used occasionally for the claim or
purpose which controls a man's action, arising from
something external, defined more precisely by the
genitivus auctoris. ὁ νόμος τῆς ἁμαρτίας = the evil purpose
forced upon me by sin (Rom. vii.25, viii.2)[3]; on the
other hand ὁ νόμος τοῦ πνεύματος τῆς ζωῆς (Rom.
viii.2) and ὁ νόμος τοῦ Χριστοῦ (Gal. vi.2) are employed
in both cases as types in contrast to the OT law. Rom.

view which lies behind this, cf. Lev. r 16, 4 on Simeon ben Azzai
who 'sat and expounded and strung the words of the Torah on to
the words of the prophets and the words of the prophets on to those
of the writings. Fire flamed up round about him and the words of
the Torah rejoiced as on the day when they were given at Sinai';
cf. Glatzer, op. cit (p. 70, n. 3), p. 38.

[1] Deut. xxviii.49 admittedly is added.
[2] Schlatter, op. cit, (p. 102, n. 2), ad loc. takes a different view.
[3] cf. also similarly Rom. vii.23.

xiii.8 is also of interest; here ὁ ἕτερος νόμος seems to allude to the summary of the law in the twofold commandment of love. For this reason ἐντολή, normally used elsewhere for a single command, has probably been avoided.

3. What Paul understands the law to mean[1]

(a) It is the cross of Jesus which determines for Paul his understanding of the content of the law. The whole of Paul's thought revolves round the proposition that the crucified Jesus is the Christ. In the same way it determines his attitude to the law. This alone provides an intelligible, inherently necessary, connexion between his affirmation and negation of the law. Otherwise only two dissimilar series of ideas could be worked out, a conservative-affirmative one and a negative-radical one.[2] For Paul the negation of the law follows from the cross: Gal. ii.21: εἰ γὰρ διὰ νόμου δικαιοσύνη, ἄρα Χριστὸς δωρεὰν ἀπέθανεν (cf Rom. vii.1 ff., viii.1 ff.)[3] It is owing to the particular nature and to the operation of the law that this proved the only way in which freedom from the law could be achieved.

(b) The nature of the law is summed up in the statement: the law is the good purpose of God. Not to be subject to the law is therefore enmity towards God (Rom. viii.7).

Paul does not make any fundamental distinction as regards content between for example the cultic and the ethical commands, or between the Decalogue and the rest of the law. Nevertheless he develops his position

1 cf. P. Bläser, *Das Gesetz bei Paulus = N.t.liche Abhandlungen*, 19 (1941); Ch. Maurer, *Die Gesetzeslehre des Paulus nach ihrem Ursprung und in ihrer Entfaltung dargelegt* (1941).
2 Michel, pp. 190 f.; cf. also A. Schweitzer, *Die Mystik des Apostel Paulus* (1930), pp. 184 f.
3 cf. O. Pfleiderer, *Der Paulinismus* (²1890), pp. 6 f., 93.

especially in relation to the ethical commands, in
particular to the commandments of the Decalogue
which are applicable to all mankind.[1] This is characteristic just because it is not done on principle.

Because the law is the proclamation of God's purpose,
it is directed towards what man does. When citing the
sentence in Lev. xviii.5: ὁ ποιήσας αὐτὰ ζήσεται ἐν αὐτοῖς
in Gal. iii.12, Rom. x.5, Paul feels the emphasis to be
on ποιεῖν.

The strictures on the Jew in Rom. ii.17 ff. make the
same assumption. The Jew certainly knows the law,
indeed his whole make-up and attitude is that of one
who possesses truth and knowledge through the law
(Rom. ii.20),[2] but he does not practise it. Yet the
aim of the law was that man should render obedience.
This is not done simply by knowing and recognising
the law. So when Paul is describing existence under
the law, he does not take as an example the man who
rejects the law, but the one who wants to keep it, who
assents to it, but yet, because he does not fulfil it, is
condemned by it.

In the case of the law it is a matter of ἔργα in contrast to πίστις with which ἀκοή is associated (Gal.
iii.2 ff.). In the life under the law it is only action
according to the law which makes a man to be religious.
To live in the law means to base one's life on keeping
the law, Gal. iii.10: εἶναι ἐξ ἔργων νόμου, and Rom.
ii.23: ἐν νόμῳ καυχᾶσθαι means to have one's reputation
in the sight of God from the law and from fulfilling the

---

[1] Paul regards the fulfilment of the law through the Spirit in the
believer as the real purpose of the law, and this view governs his
understanding of the law when judging the position of the sinner
before the law. The purpose of the law is obedience to God and
love of one's neighbour. But Paul calls the Jews to repentance on
the basis of the law as it actually is, and not of theoretical considerations.

[2] cf. Schlatter, *op. cit.* (p. 102, n. 2), *ad loc.*

law. Thus to be bound to the law is regarded by Paul as the really characteristic mark of the Jew.[1]

When Paul nevertheless says of the law that it cannot give life (Gal. iii.21), it is because no one carries it out, not by any means because perhaps Paul considers the works of the law to be sin.[2] When works of the law are done amongst the Gentiles by nature, Paul recognises them as good works (Rom. ii.14).

Hence Paul considers the law, not in the first place as revelation, God's giving of Himself, although it is the chief prerogative of the Jew that the λόγια τοῦ θεοῦ have been entrusted to him (Rom. iii.2; cf. Rom. ix.4 f.). The fact that a man knows the law still does not mean for him participation with God. Only when he carries it out, is he justified before God (Rom. ii.13).[3] Within the sphere of the law, God governs his behaviour to man by that of man towards the law.[4] So it is just from here that the new message starts, and not by criticising the law for its regulations.[5]

Paul considers that what the law demands and 'the good' are the same. This does not mean that the law derives its authority only from the fact that it is obviously good, but that a man's wrongdoing is equivalent to the Jew's transgressing of the law. In the same way knowledge of what is good is equivalent to acquaintance with the law.

---

[1] Ἰουδαῖος is synonymous with ὑπὸ νόμου εἶναι in I Cor. ix.20 ff.; cf. Lohmeyer, pp. 22 f.; cf. also TWNT III, pp. 382 ff., on Paul's use of the term Ἰουδαῖος.

[2] cf. Schlatter, *Theologie der Apostel* (²1922), p. 281.

[3] Contrary to G. Kuhlmann, *Theologia naturalis bei Philon und bei Paulus* (1930), pp. 114 ff.; K. Barth, *Der Römerbrief* (⁶1929), on Rom. ii.

[4] cf. H. Asmussen, *Theologische-kirchliche Erwägungen zum Galaterbrief* (1935): no. 188 on iii, 10 ff.; Schlatter, *op. cit.* (p. 102, n. 2), on x.5. Lohmeyer, pp. 31, 49.

[5] cf. Schlatter, *Theologie der Apostel*, 289 ff.

This becomes particularly clear when Rom. ii.6 is placed beside Rom. ii.12 ff. The ἔργον ἀγαθόν in verse 7 and the κατεργάζεσθαι τὸ κακόν in verse 9 are judged by the same yardstick as the 'being a ποιητὴς νόμου' or the ἐν νόμῳ ἁμαρτάνειν in verses 12 f. Hence this does not mean that the Jew may neglect the actual law in favour of something good which he possesses and must do,[1] but that the Gentile cannot be excused, although he is not acquainted with the law. Alternatively it is a matter of giving reasons for the statement: οὐ γάρ ἐστιν προσωπολημψία παρὰ τῷ θεῷ in Rom. ii.11. God gives his verdict on the sin of Gentiles also according to what is right. It is significant that Paul does not bring forward in support of this the rabbinic theory that the law was once delivered to all nations. He appeals instead to the assent of men to the verdict of καθῆκον (Rom. i.28). He appeals also to their awareness that the μὴ καθήκοντα named in Rom. i.29 f. are worthy of death (Rom. i.32) and to their knowledge of what it is good to do which shows itself both in the phenomenon of the conscience[2] which judges an action, and in the phenomenon of the ethical discussion[3] (Rom. ii.15).

Nevertheless men alien from the faith in Christ are differentiated in the main by the possession of the law.[4] Hence different arguments are used in Rom. ii, in verses 12 ff. for those who do not possess the law and in verses 17 ff. for those who do (cf. also Rom. iii.1 ff.,

[1] Lohmeyer, p. 32. The demands of the law and the 'good' are also equated in Rom. vii.19, 22.

[2] The conscience is not brought forward in Rom. ii.11 as a source of advice on ethics, but as a court of justice for judging actions. Cf. W. Gutbrod, *Die paulinische Anthropologie* (1934), pp. 55 f.; Schlatter, *op. cit.* (p. 102, n. 2), on ii.15.

[3] That is the point of the sentence: μεταξὺ ἀλλήλων τῶν λογισμῶν κατηγορούντων ἢ καὶ ἀπολογουμένων.

[4] cf. Brandt, p. 26.

ix.4 f.; Gal. ii.15). But just at the point which is
decisive for Paul, Jews and Gentiles now after all draw
closer together, for neither can be justified by their
keeping of the law or by some other form of goodness,
because they have all sinned (Rom. iii.23). So both
alike are dependent on faith in Christ alone, and in this
are bound together in unity (Gal. iii.28 *et passim*).
For one God stands over both parts of mankind (Rom.
iii.29 f.).

(*c*) Now this understanding of the law explains also
its effect when it comes into contact with sinful man.

(i) The relationship of the law to sin is firstly quite
simply that it forbids. The law's prohibition of sin
expresses negatively the fact that the law is the good
purpose of God. It says for example in Rom. vii.7:
οὐκ ἐπιθυμήσεις. The question in Rom. vi.15 probably
cannot be understood completely if it is not taken for
granted that the law is a defence against sin; in that
case the question is whether sin is not unavoidable if
the law is abolished.[1] Thus Paul adhered on the whole
to the firmly negative nature of the law, as well as to
the negative form of the Decalogue. The law is God's
word addressed to sin. Admittedly the law is summarised positively in the statement: ἀγαπήσεις τὸν
πλησίον σου ὡς σεαυτόν (Rom. xiii.9; Gal. v.14). But
this does not alter the fact that to start with the law
forbids τῷ πλησίον κακὸν ἐργάζεσθαι (Rom. xiii.10) as
a sin.

(ii) The law by forbidding sin at the same time reveals it. Sin is revealed in its sinfulness and its nature
as rebellion against God is made clear by the law. Sin
is indeed already there before man comes in touch
with the law (Rom. v.13, vii.9), but through the law
it springs to life: ἐλθούσης δὲ τῆς ἐντολῆς ἡ ἁμαρτία

[1] cf. Schlatter, *op. cit.* (p. 102, n. 2), *ad loc.*; on this also Schlatter,
ib. on xiii.8 f.

ἀνέζησεν (Rom. vii.9). Through the command, sin produces lust (Rom. vii.8). Thus Rom. vii.7 can mean that through the law sin first became a reality for me and does not simply become known to me.[1] Perhaps too the sentence in Rom. iv.15: οὗ δὲ οὐκ ἔστιν νόμος οὐδὲ παράβασις is to be understood in the same sense, namely that it is the law which really turns sin into rebellion.[2] Rom. v.20 is quite unequivocal: νόμος δὲ παρεισῆλθεν ἵνα πλεονάσῃ τὸ παράπτωμα (cf. Gal. iii.19); or . . . ἵνα γένηται καθ᾽ ὑπερβολὴν ἁμαρτωλὸς ἡ ἁμαρτία δία τῆς ἐντολῆς (Rom. vii.13). Paul can actually call this effect of the law its purpose (Rom. v.20; Gal. iii.19), because no effect of the law can come about apart from the divine purpose. It is true that thereby the statement that the law procures life for him who keeps it has an air of unreality; so there must always be added to it in thought an emphatic 'only'.[3]

(iii) When it is said that by the law sin is forbidden and intensified to actual rebellion against God, the condemnation of sin is pronounced at the same time. ἁμαρτία δὲ οὐκ ἐλλογεῖται μὴ ὄντος νόμου (Rom. v.13). The fact of transgressing the law, of rebelling against God places man under the κατάκριμα (Rom. viii.1). In fact the law does not only signify the condemnation of sin in practice, but also as scripture declares this condemnation and demands submission to this verdict. In Rom. iii.19 the law speaks in the manner described in Rom. iii.10 ff.: ἵνα πᾶν στόμα φραγῇ καὶ ὑπόδικος γένηται πᾶς ὁ κόσμος τῷ θεῷ. Rom. ii.12 reads: ὅσοι ἐν νόμῳ ἥμαρτον, διὰ νόμου κριθήσονται. Thus the law turns sin

[1] cf. W. G. Kümmel, *Röm. vii und die Bekehrung des Paulus* (1929), pp. 44 ff.

[2] Unless this sentence is to be explained with Schlatter, *op. cit.* (p. 102, n. 2), *ad loc.*, as meaning the abolition of the law brought about in Christ and therewith the abolition of guilt.

[3] The fact that the purpose of the law is to intensify sin, can be understood and endured only when the end of the law is in sight.

into a deadly power (I Cor. xv.56; Rom. vii.9 f.), for it produces wrath (Rom. iv.15). By this means the law leads him who listens to it aright to the knowledge of sin (Rom. iii.20)[1] (perhaps Rom. vii.7 is also to be understood in this sense). Paul is, it is true, not really concerned with this in the sense that by the knowledge made possible for him by sin man receives a subjective insight into his need for salvation, but in the sense that there is no appeal to the law before God, since it is just this which unmasks man as a sinner.

This is also why it is intelligible that Paul finds no room for the attempt to make amends for deeds transgressing the law by means of deeds fulfilling the law. By transgression, rebellion against God takes place and God's judgement is provoked. This unifies the concept of sin; sin is no longer the adding together of separate offences, just as obedience can only be one whole, not the adding together of separate good deeds. By attempting to reckon up the good deeds against the bad ones man half absolves himself from God's demands and by this endeavour transforms the nature of obedience into its opposite.

(iv) As a result of all this, the real effect of the law is to keep a man subject to his sin. As the prison holds the prisoner captive, as the παιδαγωγός keeps the boy under his authority, so man is locked up by the law under sin—and this happens according to the verdict of the law, which means according to the purpose of God (Gal. iii.22 ff.). Thus the law, rightly understood, simply prevents man's every effort to obtain righteousness in the sight of God in any other way than by faith in Christ Jesus, through the forgiving grace of God. This is different from the way promised to Abraham,

---

[1] This passage takes no account of the question whether in fact the law can or must lead man to this knowledge even without faith in Christ.

precisely because it holds a man to be responsible for his sin. According to Paul this is the actual connexion between the law and Christ. For the law is not primarily that which leads to Christ by creating the awareness of the need for redemption.

The law has this effect only because it constrains a man by the authority of God. Every challenge can give rise to awareness of human imperfection. But only God's good purpose creates the position of a man lawfully condemned before Him, whether man rejects this purpose or acknowledges it and desires to carry it out (Rom. vii.7).

(v) This describes what Paul calls the weakness of the law. It lies essentially in the fact that it cannot deal with sin otherwise than by prohibition and condemnation. The law is weak διὰ τῆς σαρκός (Rom. viii.3) owing to the fact of sin which the law cannot overcome. Thus the weakness of the law can also be expressed by saying that it is not capable of making alive (Gal. iii.21). Indeed on the contrary through sin it produces death (Rom. vii.9 f.; I Cor. xv.56). Moreover this is also intended when the law as the letter which kills is contrasted with the spirit which gives life (II Cor. iii.6 ff.). It is a splendid duty to serve the law written on tables of stone, for it is the revealed purpose of God. But its effect is condemnation and death, because it approaches man from the outside and does not stir him from the centre of his being. It lets him go on living as the sinner that he is; indeed it holds him fast to this sin, without its being possible to remove this sin from him. Thus II Cor. iii.6 contains substantially the same idea as for instance Rom. vii or Gal. iii, and does not convey the contrast between the religion of the letter and the religion of conviction which has been a favourite interpretation of this verse.

The fact that Paul perceived the effect of the law in

this way is perhaps expressed most clearly by his inclusion of it amongst the στοιχεῖα τοῦ κόσμου (Gal. iv.3, 9; Col. ii.8, 20). The meaning of this term is brought out most clearly in Col. ii. 20: He who dies with Christ to the στοιχεῖα τοῦ κόσμου should not submit to orders as though he were still ἐν κόσμῳ. In Gal. iv.3, 9 too the emphasis no doubt rests on κόσμος. The law is something which belongs to the characteristic permanent substance of this world[1] and therefore cannot lead beyond this condition and give release from bondage to sin. Yet this weakness of the law exists not in spite of, but on account of its holiness as a revelation of the purpose of God with which it confronts men (cf. Rom. vii.14).

(d) This radical understanding of the law by Paul is intelligible only with his spiritual point of departure in mind, namely that the act of forgiveness and justification is accomplished by the cross of Christ and by this means man's relationship to God is established anew by him, apart from man's achievement and hence apart from the law. Paul's negation of the law springs from his affirmation of what has taken place in Jesus Christ, and not from a judgement based on reason nor from missionary tactics. Righteousness before God was bestowed on man through the cross not on account of what man did, but because he was taken up in mercy into this death, that is to say, through faith. For this reason the negation is necessary (Rom. iii.21 ff.). Hence it is Paul's aim to be found in Christ: μὴ ἔχων ἐμὴν δικαιοσύνην τὴν ἐν νόμου, ἀλλὰ τὴν διὰ πίστεως Χριστοῦ, τὴν ἐκ θεοῦ δικαιοσύνην (Phil. iii.9). οὐδὲν ἄρα νῦν κατάκριμα τοῖς ἐν Χριστῷ Ἰησοῦ (Rom. viii.1).

But apart from the death of Christ and from death in

[1] cf. M. Dibelius, *Die Geisterwelt im Glauben des Paulus* (1909), p. 84.

Christ, man is still ἐν κόσμῳ and hence handed over to
the law (Col. ii.20). So the sentence in Rom. x.4:
τέλος γὰρ νόμου Χριστὸς εἰς δικαιοσύνην παντὶ τῷ πιστεύοντι,
does not simply mean that the period of the law is over
with the coming of Christ, that the law and Christ
succeed each other in temporal history, nor even in
religious history, but in 'salvation-history'. Only when
a man lets himself appropriate the righteousness of
God in Christ, is the law abolished for him. Paul
expresses this by saying that removal from the sphere
of the law takes place only by dying (Rom. vii.1 ff.;
Gal. ii.19; Col. ii.20). Now this dying is nothing other
than having a share in Christ's death: ἐθανατώθητε
τῷ νόμῳ διὰ τοῦ σώματος τοῦ Χριστοῦ (Rom. vii.4);
Χριστῷ συνεσταύρωμαι (Gal. ii.19); ἀπεθάνετε σὺν Χριστῷ
(Col. ii.20). Beside this there stands baptism into
Christ, through which we are sons of God and no
longer slaves and hence no longer subjected to the law
(Gal. iii towards the end). In Rom. vi baptism and
death with Christ are again combined.[1] Now all this
means simply that the relationship with God now rests
no longer with man himself. Thus the law as the road
to salvation is now barred; Christ has stepped into its
place. Therefore man is now forbidden to desire still
to become righteous through the law after God has
revealed himself in Jesus Christ as the one who for-
gives, who justifies the sinner and not the man who is
just by his own efforts (Rom. iv.5). Consequently
he who still expects righteousness from the fulfilment of the law has caused Christ to die in vain (Gal.
ii.21).

(e) The positive connexion between the law and
Christ is preserved by understanding the cross as an
affirmation of the law. Firstly, it affirms its verdict.
Dying to the law, being crucified together with Christ

[1] cf. Gutbrod, pp. 190 ff.

happens precisely διὰ νόμου (Gal. ii.19).[1] Gal. iii.13
makes this still clearer: Χριστὸς ἡμᾶς ἐξηγόρασεν ἐκ τῆς
κατάρας τοῦ νόμου γενόμενος ὑπερ ἡμῶν κατάρα (cf.
II Cor. v.21: *Christ was made to be sin for us*); and so the
law's sentence of condemnation on sin reached its
fulfilment in the cross of Christ (Rom. v.6 ff.). This is
not in fact worked out explicitly in this sense in Paul's
writings, but it follows from the logic of the argument
that the cross of Christ is also the fulfilment of the law
in so far as the law's cardinal purpose came to fulfilment in the cross. The cross is the consummation of
obedience to God (Phil. ii.5 ff.), and at the same time
it is love to men made perfect (Rom. viii.34). After all
just this is the real purpose of the law. Thus it is also
disobedience to the law to desire it to be different from
this, its fulfilment. To state that here the law is fulfilled and to emphasise this fact is not Paul's present
purpose, for otherwise the primacy of the law would
have lain very near; but it was very much to his
purpose to show how faith in Christ brings the law to
fulfilment in the believer.

Through faith alone a complete recognition of the
verdict implicit in the law is reached, whilst the attempt
to be justified through the works of the law necessarily
weakens the verdict or renders it ineffective. This is
why Rom. i-iii and Rom. vii were written. But the
new obedience has its roots in dying with Christ, in
whom the relationship to God has been established
apart from the law by God's act (Rom. vi.11 ff.), and
by the same process the fruit of the Spirit springs up by
faith (Gal. v.22). The law attains its fulfilment, at
any rate negatively in the first place, by its condemnation not being challenged (Gal. v.23). This is true

[1] Zahn, *Galater* ([3]1922), *ad loc.* interprets this διὰ νόμου thus:
because the law showed me my need for redemption and referred
me to faith.

because its demands can be summed up in the command to love (Gal. v.14; Rom. xiii.10). In fact the twofold command to love (probably referring to Jesus in Matt. xxii.36 ff.) can be called simply the νόμος so that the command to love one's neighbour is ὁ ἕτερος νόμος (Rom. xiii.8); ὁ νόμος τοῦ Χριστοῦ in Gal. vi.2 no doubt means the same thing. Thus the real purpose of the law is fulfilled in the case of the man who has been taken up into love through Christ. Rom. viii.4: ἵνα τὸ δικαίωμα τοῦ νόμου πληρωθῇ ἐν ἡμῖν τοῖς μὴ κατὰ σάρκα περιπατοῦσιν ἀλλὰ κατὰ πνεῦμα. Paul can therefore say in Rom. iii.31 not only that through the gospel of justi-fication by faith is the law not abolished, but that it is really upheld for the first time, and as a matter of fact the law in this passage is used not in the sense of making a promise (cf. Rom. iv), nor as condemning (cf. Rom. iii.10 ff.), but in its specific sense of giving commands.

Now by the acceptance of Jesus' death in faith, the law is brought to its fulfilment in accordance with its real purpose, namely union with God in obedience and love of one's neighbour. But in addition Paul recognises as well the fulfilment of the actual OT law from love and from obedience. It is true that he takes his stand primarily against any attempt to demand this fulfilment of the OT law, and equally that of a Christian rule, with the idea that it is necessary in order to be justified before God.[1] But he was ready himself to observe the Mosaic law in order to further the gospel amongst the Jews (I Cor. ix.20 ff.). Indeed he can advise one born a Jew not to remove the marks of circumcision (I Cor. vii.18 ff.). This does not mean that Paul retreats from his doctrine of justification into a 'legal' way of thinking, but that he is thoroughly

---

[1] Thus in particular Gal. ii.3 ff. on the conflict about the circumcision of Titus; also Gal. ii.11 ff. in the controversy with Peter.

I

consistent in his teaching about justification and in his
preaching about freedom in Christ, since man can now
even refrain from making use of his freedom for the
sake of his love towards a weaker brother, or perhaps
to build up the community, or because he just happens
to be in a particular position. He is in no way justified
because he carries out the law and makes use of his
knowledge and the freedom he has obtained by it. On
the contrary, his only claim is that he is known by God
(I Cor. viii.3).

Finally Paul uses the law in addition in order to find
in it guidance for the actual life of the community, that
is to say, in the διδαχή. In I Cor. ix.8 f.; xiv.21, 34 the
law is employed to supply by allegorical exegesis an
answer (or, as the case may be, a confirmation of the
answer already discussed) to questions concerning the
community life. But it is noteworthy here that the
argument from the law is not adduced as the decisive
proof, but as the confirmation of what has been already
recognised as right from other considerations.[1] The
OT is not understood here to be a law to be obeyed;
it has not the weight attached in Judaism to an appeal
to the law. Moreover on the whole this use of the law
plays no great part.[2] At any rate when the community
conducts itself as the law requires, this behaviour is not
to be justified merely by appeal to the law. For only
that is considered right and must be respected which
is the outcome of obedience to Christ in faith, according
to the measure of faith given to each one (Rom. xiv.1 ff.,
xii.3). Sin is no longer that which does not proceed
from the law, but that which does not proceed from
faith (Rom. xiv.23).

[1] This shown by the καί in I Cor. xiv.34 and I Cor. ix.8.
[2] cf. the absence of νόμος in Rom. xii ff. (except in xiii.8 ff.;
but here the actual law itself is replaced by the command to love).
Moreover it is absent in Thessalonians and II Corinthians.

(*f*) No simple answer can be given to the question as to the origin of this understanding of the law by Paul. There is no sufficient basis in exegesis for the theory that his own painful experience when faced by the demands of the law[1] and his sense of unworthiness with regard to the law led Paul to hold this view of it.[2] On the one hand this is not required by Rom. vii, and on the other it is made practically impossible by Phil. iii.6: κατὰ δικαιοσύνην τὴν ἐν νόμῳ γενόμενος ἄμεμπτος.

Yet it is a fact that for Paul the point of view from which he regards his attitude to the law is determined decisively by his faith in the divine revelation which took place on the cross of Christ. This raises the more precise question, as to how far his doctrine concerning the law really sprang from the consistent working out of his faith in the crucified as it affected the law, or how far it was only the criterion by which to accept or reject those solutions and answers regarding the problem of the law which were already championed before him and around him. This is not the place in which to supply the answer to this question.

At all events Paul had from the beginning a penetrating view of the contrast between the way of the law and that of faith.[3] Indeed he had probably already before his conversion seen in the law the line of cleavage between Judaism and Christianity. A gradual development of his understanding of the law either in the

---

[1] Thus e.g. Grafe, pp. 13 ff. In Gal. ii.16 too the εἰδότες does not suggest that this knowledge was brought about as a result of experience.

[2] This theory arose mainly through transferring the course of Luther's development to that of Paul. Cf. Lietzmann on Gal. vii; for a criticism, Lohmeyer, pp. 5 ff.

[3] cf. Schlatter, *Geschichte des ersten Christentums*, p. 127. Certainly Gal. v.11 may not be understood as a backward glance at a Christian ministry by Paul in which he required circumcision as necessary to salvation.

direction of tightening it up[1] or toning it down[2] is in
any case not probable for the crucial points.[3]

C. *The Period after the conflict concerning the law*

1. *The Letter to the Hebrews*

νόμος is used in Hebrews with a meaning similar to
that used elsewhere in the NT. As a rule it is the OT
law. Only in vii.16 is it open to question whether the
translation should not be more generally 'rule' or
'ordinance'[4]; but as this is the only passage in the letter,
it would be better to explain it here too as the OT law.
ἐντολῆς σαρκίνης would in that case no doubt have to be
understood as a genitive expressing the content,[5] i.e.
according to the law concerning bodily commandments.
The plural of νόμος appears indeed twice in Hebrews,
but only in quotations (viii.10, x.16). As in the case
of Paul, there is no basic difference between ὁ νόμος
and νόμος. Even vii.12, for example, is not intended to
be a generally valid rule, but applies only to the OT
law in particular. Perhaps sometimes its subject-
matter does not include the whole OT law, but in the
first instance that part of it concerned with the ministry
of the priests and the priesthood, for example ix.22:
σχεδὸν ἐν αἵματι πάντα καθαρίζεται κατὰ τὸν νόμον. But
in no case is there intended to be a fundamental distinction. Just when it is contrasted with ἐντολή as the
single commandment, νόμος does usually mean the
OT law as a whole (e.g. vii.5).

(*a*) The fact that the meaning of νόμος tends to be
the law ordering the ministry of the priests is due to

----

[1] Thus C. Clemen, *Die Chronologie der paulinischen Briefe* (1893),
especially pp. 256 ff.; but cf. ThLZ (1902)No. 8, col. 233.

[2] Thus Sieffert in: *Theologische Studien ... B. Weiss ... dargebracht*
(1897). [3] cf. Juncker, pp. 171 ff.; Grafe, pp. 27 ff.

[4] Thus e.g. F. Bleek, *Der Brief an die Hebräer* II, 2(1840) *ad loc.*

[5] cf. Blass, *Grammatik des neutestl. Griechisch*, ed. Debrunner,
ed. 6, § 167. (Cf. above p. 103, n. 1.)

this being the chief concern of the letter. The point of view from which the law is regarded in Hebrews is essentially different from, for example, that of Jesus or Paul. By them the law is seen as the purpose of God which requires and controls a man's actions, which aims at works, and gives life to him who puts it into practice. In Hebrews on the contrary the law is treated as that which gives to the priesthood its underlying principle, its dignity and its importance. It has a share in the nature and efficacy of this priestly ministry, and so this nature and efficacy depend on the fact that it is based on the law.[1] This means of course at the same time that the theme of Hebrews is not concerned with the relationship between law and gospel, but with that between the OT ministry of the priests and the priestly ministry and priesthood of Jesus. The comparison is extended to the law only in so far as the efficacy of the OT priests' ministry is due to its being founded on the law.

How much the fact of its being anchored to the law contributes to the importance of the OT priesthood[2] is shown not only by the frequent emphatic κατὰ τὸν νόμον or κατὰ νόμον in vii.5, viii.4, x.8,[3] but especially by some passages giving technical arguments.

The glory of Christ's priesthood depends upon this very circumstance that he is not a priest κατὰ νόμον ἐντολῆς σαρκίνης but κατὰ δύναμιν ζωῆς ἀκαταλύτου (vii.16). But this cannot do away with the fact that in

[1] Admittedly in x.28 νόμος also occurs with the meaning usual elsewhere: *he who violates the law must die; how much more he who has spurned the Son of God!* Cf. also ii.2. But these passages simply demonstrate the fact that the problem concerning the duty of obeying the actual law has ceased to exist. On this question cf. Brandt, pp. 34 f.

[2] cf. Th. Haering, *Der Brief an die Hebräer* (1925), pp. 62 ff.

[3] κατά passes here from the sense of 'according to', 'in the manner of' to that of 'in the strength of', and almost that of 'through'.

these statements the holiness of the law is recognised.[1]

(b) Although the OT priesthood derives its strength and authority from the law, it cannot produce the τελείωσις (vii.11). Therefore the same can be said of the law as well, on which the life of the priesthood depends: οὐδὲν γὰρ ἐτελείωσεν ὁ νόμος (vii.19).

The aim of the priestly ministry should really be to bring man near to God (vii.19), the τελείωσις and its prerequisite the καθαρίζειν τὴν συνείδησιν ἀπὸ νεκρῶν ἔργων εἰς τὸ λατρεύειν θεῷ ζῶντι (ix.14), in short ἀφαιρεῖν ἁμαρτίας (x.4).[2] This aim is summed up for instance in ix.28 or x.19 ff. For it is just that crucial part of what is bestowed on the believer through the true High Priest Christ to which the law and the priesthood depending on it could not attain, or could do so only inadequately.

The reason for this weakness and uselessness (ἀσθενὲς καὶ ἀνωφελές, vii.18) on account of which it could not attain to its object, is expounded in vii.18 ff., and this is again summed up in vii.28 in the antithesis: ὁ νόμος γὰρ ἀνθρώπους καθίστησιν ἀρχιερεῖς ἔχοντας ἀσθένειαν, ὁ λόγος δὲ τῆς ὁρκωμοσίας τῆς μετὰ τὸν νόμον υἱὸν εἰς τὸν αἰῶνα τετελειωμένον. Thus the weakness of the law and consequently of the OT priesthood lies essentially in

[1] The Epistle of Barnabas affords a typical contrast to this. In it the allegorical exegesis of the OT pointing to Christ leads even to the assertion that the actual carrying out of the commandments of the OT, for instance circumcision, is to be ascribed to the seduction of an evil angel (ix.4), since the commandment was from the beginning never intended to be carried out literally. Moreover in x.2: *So then it is not a commandment of God that they should not bite with their teeth* (i.e. the animals forbidden in the law), *but Moses spoke it in the spirit* (cf. x.9). This is a continuing development of the Hellenistic disintegration of the OT law in the manner of the Letter of Aristeas and Philo. In Hebrews this is simply not there, in spite of some formal similarities.

[2] As a matter of fact, sacrifice is looked upon in Hebrews mainly as expiation (v.1). Cf. Haering, pp. 42 f.

the weakness of the men with whom the law has
to do.

This weakness is seen in the mortal nature of the
priests (vii.24 ff.) and especially in the fact that they
must always first offer a sacrifice for themselves, that
is to say, that they are themselves bound up with sin
(vii.27: v.3). Connected with this is the fact that the
OT sacrifice cleanses merely externally, not from
within; this does away neither with the consciousness
of guilt nor with the sin itself (ix.9 f.). Hence, since the
law and its priesthood has to do with sinful men, it
cannot carry out its task; it cannot procure for men
access to the Holy of Holies, to God.

We may summarise the point thus: according to
Paul the law is weak because men do *not* do it, whilst
according to Hebrews it is so because it is *men* who do
it. The two statements start from different guiding
principles, but fundamentally they both contain the
same verdict. The close connexion between them is
seen in Hebrews by the use of Jer. xxxi.31 ff. where the
frailty of the old covenant is shown up by Israel's
violation of it. It is seen too in the fact that Jesus'
priestly ministry sanctifies better than the old one
because it is based on the sacrifice of obedience which
is well pleasing to God (x.5 ff.).

(*c*) At this point we find in Hebrews too the peculiar
turn of thought found in Paul. The verdict is pronounced in the light of the fulfilment,[1] and this verdict
is that the law not only could not reach its goal, but
also ought not to do so. On the contrary the law points
to Christ just because it holds man fast in sinfulness in
order to let him find access to God by the one manner

---

[1] In Hebrews too the verdict on the insufficiency of the old
worship of God does not issue from a rational criticism of it,
although sentences like ix.12a at first sound very much like this,
but from the fact of Jesus' High-priesthood, viii.1 ff., 10 ff.

proclaimed through the scripture, namely through the high-priestly ministry of Jesus alone. For the sacrifice offered in accordance with the law was the ἀνάμνησις ἁμαρτιῶν κατ' ἐνιαυτόν (x.3), for the law has not the εἰκὼν τῶν πραγμάτων, but only the σκιὰ τῶν μελλόντων ἀγαθῶν (x.1).[1] So it was only with the new covenant of which Christ is the mediator that there could be a blotting out of τῶν ἐπὶ τῇ πρώτῃ διαθήκῃ παραβάσεων and a receiving of the promise (ix.15). Thus the eternal High-priesthood of Christ, which existed already before the law and was from the beginning above[2] the law, was announced by the figure of Melchizedek and was declared with an oath in Ps. cx to belong to Christ. This High-priesthood means not only the μετάθεσις νόμου (vii.5), but at the same time the fulfilment, the εἰκὼν τῶν πραγμάτων instead of only the temporary σκιὰ τῶν μελλόντων ἀγαθῶν (x.1).[3]

(d) In spite of all the differences from the Pauline understanding of the law, the strong resemblance is striking, particularly in the manner in which the old and new covenants are placed in relationship to each other, and the abrogation and the fulfilment of the old one by the new one are intertwined. Whether there are indeed direct Pauline influences here cannot be decided from these considerations. At any rate when comparing them we must observe that in Hebrews there is no question, or perhaps rather no longer any question, of the attempt to find in the law a demand for good actions to justify men. This circumstance links Hebrews in regard to the problem of the law more closely with John and James than with Paul.

[1] These good things are 'to come', no doubt from the standpoint of the law.
[2] This is the meaning of the elaborate proof that Levi paid tithes to Melchizedek in Abraham (vii.5 ff.).
[3] cf. Brandt, p. 40.

2. *The Letter of James*

The decisions on the questions as to when and by whom this letter was written and the interpretation of its understanding of the law are mutually dependent.[1] Unfortunately it must be admitted that there is not enough material to be quite sure of the interpretation. Yet two facts stand out. First the question of the relationship of faith and works is posed and answered without any reference to the law (ii.14 ff.). The subject is definitely the relationship of faith and works, not, as with Paul and his opponents, that of faith and law.

It is true that these questions overlap to a considerable extent, but they are not necessarily identical. Certainly ii.14 ff. is an attack on a misunderstood Paul,[2] but not in the name of the law, nor only with reference to the law, but in the name of showing faith in practice by works, by deeds of love (ii.16).

Second, where mention is made of νόμος, a qualifying phrase is often added: νόμος τέλειος τῆς ἐλευθερίας in i.25, νόμος ἐλευθερίας in ii.12, νόμοι βασιλικός in ii.8, which is evidently intended each time (or at least in the first two cases) to contrast what is meant here with some other meaning described by νόμος alone. Both these points probably indicate a time when the discussion of the primitive community about the law is still known, but a decision has already been made against the law.[3] The real danger is seen to be no longer either keeping the law or pushing it aside, but understanding faith in a wrong way, such as might derive from the Pauline answer to that question. This is completely

---

[1] cf. Dibelius, *Der Brief des Jakobus*, ed. Greeven ([9]1957), p. 15.

[2] We can leave the question open here whether the writer himself misunderstood Paul in this way or is only attacking a misunderstanding of this kind which owed its origin to Paul.

[3] cf. J. Marty, *L'Épitre de Jacques* (1935), pp. 248, 60; Dibelius, *Jakobus* on i.25 and ii.8.

independent of whether the writer is a Jew or not. (That he is one, appears almost conclusively from his style.)[1]

This general situation must explain those passages in which the law is mentioned: i.25, ii.8 ff., iv.11 ff.

(a) In i.25 the νόμος τέλειος τῆς ἐλευθερίας is substantially the same as, or at any rate belongs to, the λόγος ἔμφυτος δυνάμενος σῶσαι τὰς ψυχάς in verse 21, and παρακύψαι εἰς νόμον is the same as δοκεῖν θρησκὸν εἶναι and as θρησκεία in verse 26. Hence here the word of God, on which the position of Christians is established, is called νόμος.[2] It is therefore defined with regard to that aspect of its nature which is concerned not merely with passive acceptance, but with determining one's life, particularly, as verse 27 indicates, in deeds of love.[3] The addition τέλειος τῆς ἐλευθερίας then guards the expression against misunderstanding, as though it meant the command of the OT law. Therefore in so far as the gospel message lays claim to a man's life with respect to his actions also, it can be called νόμος,[4] though compared with the old law it is a perfect law of liberty. But what these phrases are intended to convey more precisely, does not appear clearly from this passage.[5] But light may be thrown on it by the two other passages.

(b) In ii.8 the νόμος is in the first place evidently not

[1] The use of νόμος too with or without the article without any difference of meaning points to this.

[2] Against A. Meyer, Das Rätsel des Jakobus (1930), pp. 153 ff.

[3] It is therefore perhaps not completely apposite when Windisch Jakobusbrief, speaks of a 'reduction' of the Torah to the 'religious and moral commandments'.

[4] The phrase 'the conception of Christianity itself as a law' (Weizsäcker, p. 365, ET, II p. 27) is at the very least a misleading one.

[5] The non-Christian parallels, cf. the commentaries ad loc., do not enable us to understand this phrase so clearly as to yield an explanation by themselves. So the other statements in this letter are a better guide for exegesis.

simply another expression for the word of truth, but a command in the strict sense. The only question is whether it means the whole OT law including all its commandments, or their summary in the law of love.[1] At any rate verse 10 taken by itself can be understood to mean the whole OT law, including all its commands, represented as obligatory. Not only the attitude of the rest of the letter, however, but the context of the verse too refutes this interpretation: verse 8 says: *if you really fulfil the law of love you do well*. But then verse 9 adds: *yet if προσωπολημψία is found among you* (as it was described in ii.1 ff.) then it is a sin, and in fact just in view of this law; for only when the whole of the law is performed[2]—verse 10 can be rendered thus can one escape condemnation. In that case the law in verses 9 f. would mean simply the law of love which in verse 8 was called the royal law, and βασιλικός would then describe the nature of this law as contrasted with another understanding of it, and not this one commandment alongside others equal to it in principle.[3] If those who are addressed should perchance justify their behaviour by an appeal to the law of love, which after all includes the rich man, the letter says to them: yes, certainly, but in that case this law too must be taken quite seriously. But by προσωπολημψία the law of love is denied (in an essential point)[4] and consequently this action is condemned by the commandment.[5]

[1] It may not simply be concluded that νόμος in James means the Decalogue, just because in verse 11 two commandments of it are used to illustrate the principle in verse 10.

[2] ἐν ἑνί need not mean: one commandment of the OT, but probably has a more general meaning: *in one point, in one particular way*.

[3] Both interpretations of βασιλικός are in themselves possible according to the usage outside the NT, cf. the commentaries *ad loc*.

[4] Marty, *ad loc*.

[5] To condone evil by reason of the good that was intended or by citing the commandment is rejected here as elsewhere in the NT.

If the passage is understood in this way, then we have a consistent picture, in which only the use of νόμος in verse 11 seems a little incongruous. But after all verse 11 is adduced as an example to corroborate verse 10 and does not quite fit into the train of thought. In that case τῆς ἐλευθερίας is probably added again in verse 12 just because of the different use of νόμος in this passage, a usage which corresponds more closely to the usual one. The νόμος ἐλευθερίας of verse 12 is thus the same as the νόμος βασιλικός of verse 8, that is to say the law of love, which is 'the law' in its true sense. It is therefore the standard for judging speech and action.

Hence an inner connexion can be effected between the conception of the law expressed here and that in i.25. In so far as the word is directed to a man's action, it is the law of love, and just for this reason it is the perfect law and not the sum of particular laws.

(c) Perhaps iv.11 f. throws light on the meaning of the phrase that the law is a law of liberty. The comparison of this passage with Rom. ii.1 f. or Matt. vii.1 ff. breaks down just at the point peculiar to James iv.11 f. For here alongside the judgement of others is placed not that of myself but that of the law, and only after that my own. A comparison with Rom. xiv.4 is the most likely.[1] In that case νόμος would mean here the purpose of God which alone holds good for the individual. Another person has no insight into this as a matter of course, because this purpose of God will not let itself be enmeshed in precise, unambiguous forms and actions.[2] To condemn another man because

because man has to do, not with commandments, but with God.

[1] Weizsäcker, p. 368, ET, II p. 31.

[2] cf. also the author's designation of himself as θεοῦ καὶ κυρίου Ἰησοῦ Χριστοῦ δοῦλος in i.1; Schlatter, *Der Brief des Jakobus* (²1956), on i.25.

his actions do not agree with what I consider to be right means arrogating to myself a judgement concerning the commandment which that other man should observe. But in doing so one is no longer a doer of the law.[1] Understood in this way the passage shows how serious is the statement that from the Christian point of view the law is a law of liberty which does not tie the individual down to fixed commandments but to the obedience of love with which he has just been commissioned. Thus this freedom is freedom through the bond of obedience to God, and therefore, in spite of its being free from the individual commandments, it no more hampers ethical guidance and instruction than it does in Paul. In fact it is this sense that this letter intends to give them. Indeed it does not confine the freedom of obedience anywhere within a scheme in the manner of a law.

Thus the letter of James in its understanding of the law is altogether in the Christian line of thought which bases its understanding of the law on the obedience of faith, but temporally it is remote from the actual conflict concerning the recognition of the OT law.

3. *The Gospel according to John*

νόμος occurs rather more frequently in John than in Matthew (14:8 times). Nevertheless the actual

---

[1] Schlatter, *Jakobus*, *ad loc.* offers for consideration a similar exegesis. Another exegesis of the passage assumes that καταλαλεῖν and κρίνειν νόμον is simply an expression for 'transgressing', in which case νόμος would be the law of love (cf. Windisch, *Jakobus*, *ad loc*; similarly also Harnack, *Jakobus*, *ad loc.*). In view of verse 12 this is less likely, for the sentence which says that lawgiving and judgement are united in God surely means that only He who has also given him the commandment, has the right to pass a verdict on each man's deeds.

problem of the law does not occupy nearly so pivotal a position as it does there.

The meaning of the word νόμος is the usual one. It is the Torah, especially the Pentateuch, e.g. i.45: ἔγραψεν Μωυσῆς ἐν τῷ νόμῳ καὶ οἱ προφῆται. But it occurs also in the broader sense, namely the OT generally: x.34: what is γεγραμμένον ἐν τῷ νόμῳ ὑμῶν is a passage from the Psalms, so are xii.34, xv.25. Besides this, νόμος naturally has also the meaning of law in the actual sense, namely a command to do a particular thing, as for example in the discussion about Jesus' breaking of the sabbath in vii.19, 23. In this sense νόμος is also a legal ordinance, e.g. vii.51: μὴ ὁ νόμος ἡμῶν κρίνει τὸν ἄνθρωπον ἐάν μὴ ἀκούσῃ πρῶτον παρ' αὐτοῦ καὶ γνῷ τί ποιεῖ; or in xviii.31 in the mouth of Pilate: κατὰ τὸν νόμον ὑμῶν κρίνατε αὐτόν, or in the mouth of the Jews before Pilate in xix.7a where the indefinite form is required by the meaning.

As regards its content the chief point to notice is that the law does not particularly interest John as a possibility for the guidance or the organisation of human, or indeed of Christian, action. Even in those cases where the narrative is particularly concerned with Jesus' setting the law aside, e.g. chapters v (with vii.19 ff.) and ix, the subject of interest is not really the validity of the law, but these cases and questions provide the occasion and starting point for the development in each case of the real theme.

In John's gospel the interest lies in the first place in the law as revelation, and in this sense it is set over against Jesus.

(a) Thus we have especially i.17: ὁ νόμος διὰ Μωυσέως ἐδόθη, ἡ χάρις καὶ ἡ ἀλήθεια διὰ Ἰησοῦ Χριστοῦ ἐγένετο. This must be understood with reference to verse 18. It is only in Jesus that God is really revealed, only here in the word made flesh does God really make Himself

known, and He does so in the gift of mercy and truth[1]
(vv. 14, 17). It is in accordance with this that a series
of expressions with which Jesus designates himself, or
with which he is designated, are contrasted with corresponding statements about the Torah. Jesus, the Light
(viii.12, ix.5, xii.35), contrasted with the Torah as the
light[2]; Jesus gives the water of life (ch. iv) contrasted
with the Torah without which Israel cannot live any
more than can fish without water[3]; Jesus, the bread
of life (ch. vi); Jesus as the Way, the Truth and the
Life (xiv.6); all these are paralleled by assertions about
the Torah.[4] So too does the designation of Jesus as the
logos made flesh, together with statements about the
pre-existence and the mediating activity of this logos
in creation.

But apart from the fact that these contrasts, which
are usually implicit, by no means apply to the Torah
alone,[5] it must be observed that the parallels are not
simply due to transferring the features associated with
the Torah mechanically and point by point so as to
make christological statements. In both places, in
John and in Jewish theology, these expressions are

[1] So it is not at all a question of a criticism of the kind suggested
by W. Bauer, *Johannesevangelium* ([3]1933), on i.16: As contrasted
with the high esteem in which Moses was held by the Jews 'the
Christian criticism shows that not even the whole extent of the
law goes back to Moses, much less that his actions should be considered as real divine actions (vi.32). Hence trust placed in him
is vain.' vii.22 is inclined rather to attribute a higher dignity to
circumcision because it goes even as far back as to the patriarchs.
Nor is the conclusion drawn from vi.32 consistent with the text.

[2] Strack-Billerbeck I p. 237d; K. H. Rengstorf 'Zu den
Fresken in der jüdischen Katakombe der Villa Torlonia in Rom'
ZNW 31 (1932), pp. 52 ff.   [3] Strack-Billerbeck, II, pp. 435 f.

[4] Strack-Billerbeck, II, pp. 482 ff.; for the whole argument cf.
Bornhäuser, *Das Johannesevangelium eine Missionsschrift für Israel*
(1928); also TWNT IV, p. 139.

[5] cf Bauer, *Johannesevangelium*, ad loc.

determined by the central statement in each case: in the Torah the divine revelation is present, and in Jesus the revelation is present. Now to the extent that in non-rabbinic circles other corresponding basic theories are to be found and lead to expressions of this kind, these statements about Jesus form a rival theory to these too. At any rate so far as the Torah is concerned it is contrasted as a word of revelation with the Son as the perfect revelation.

(b) But this does not mean that the relation between them is merely that of 'either-or'. There is also a definite inner connexion between the law as the word of the scripture and the revelation of God in Jesus.[1] In the law, in scripture, Jesus is attested and promised as the Christ, i.45: ὃν ἔγραψεν Μωυσῆς ἐν τῷ νόμῳ καὶ οἱ προφῆται εὑρήκαμεν (i.e. in Jesus): similarly in v.39 f. Even though the word νόμος is lacking here, it might after all in fact be used, as is shown by the section vii.19 ff. which no doubt fits into the context of ch. v. The scriptures bear witness to Jesus. In this sense John mentions the law several times: that which the law says or even commands is fulfilled in the existence and the activity of Jesus (viii.17, x.34, xii.34, xv.25).[2]

Certainly the emphasis here is placed strongly on the critical result of this relationship: when a man

[1] E. Hirsch states in *Das vierte Evangelium in seiner ursprünglichen Gestalt verdeutscht und erklärt* (1936) that 'the basic idea of the gospel, dominating the whole of it, is the fact that between Christianity and Judaism, between faith in the word which sets free and has life and the Jewish obligations which mean servitude, there exists an irreconcilable conflict' (pp. 78 f.). With regard to this statement it is not only questionable whether this really is the dominating basic idea of the gospel, but also whether the gospel shows only an irreconcilable conflict. Cf. also R. Bultmann, 'Hirschs Auslegung des Johannesevangelium', in *Evangelische Theologie* (1937), pp. 115 ff. especially 128 ff.

[2] So it is not a question of somehow adding the OT and the word of Jesus, as Bornhäuser, p. 77, understands John ii.22.

rejects Jesus as the Christ, his appeal to the law is seen
to be rebellion against the scripture; thus especially
v. 39 ff. Genuine faith with regard to Moses and with
regard to the law, genuine listening to this revelation,
must lead to the acknowledgement of Jesus. So rejection of Jesus is at the same time rejection of the
revelation of the law. This means that the emphatic
ὁ νόμος ὁ ὑμέτερος in viii.17, and ὁ νόμος ὑμῶν in x.34
are to be understood as meaning: it is just the law to
which you appeal against me, it is just its testimony,
which applies to me; therefore if you do not hear me,
you do not hear the scripture either[1]—hence it does
not mean 'your law with which I have nothing to do'.[2]

(c) Exactly the same relationship between Jesus and
the law is shown in those passages too in which the law
is thought of as the organisation of human activities.
Firstly again in the antithesis: Jesus is bound solely to
the will of the Father, not to the commands of the law
(v.19) and accordingly the disciples are bound to the
commandment given in the Son, which takes the place
of the law for them and expresses itself in the law of
love: ἐντολὴν καινὴν δίδωμι ὑμῖν, ἵνα ἀγαπᾶτε ἀλλήλους,
. . . ἀγάπην ἔχητε ἐν ἀλλήλοις (xiii.34 f.). Verse 35 in
particular shows how for the disciples the obligation
to the Torah, for example, is replaced by their relationship to Jesus as his disciples, and this finds its appropriate expression in the law of love. Through this
relationship they are released from that of a servant
(xv.15). In Christ alone are they able to perform a
fruitful work (xv.5).

And again there stands beside it the close positive
connexion: He who genuinely carries out the law has

---

[1] cf. Zahn, *Das Evangeliun des Johannes* ([5,6]1921), on viii.17 and
x.34. Zahn no doubt rightly compares the ὑμῖν in Matt. xxii.25.
There is a greater difficulty with xv.25; yet cf. xvi.2.

[2] Thus xviii.31 in Pilate's mouth.

K

a share in Christ. Nathaniel is called to Jesus as
ἀληθῶς 'Ισραηλίτης, ἐν ᾧ δόλος οὐκ ἔστιν (i.47 ff.). No
doubt vii.17 belongs here too: ἐάν τις θέλῃ τὸ θέλημα
αὐτοῦ (sc. of God) ποιεῖν, γνώσεται περὶ τῆς διδαχῆς,
πότερον ἐκ τοῦ θεοῦ ἐστιν ἢ ἐγὼ ἀπ' ἐμαυτοῦ λαλῶ.

Now this at the same time implies the negative,
namely that the rejection of Jesus involves also the
rejection of the purpose of the law. In vii.19 the
design to kill Jesus lays bare the οὐ ποιεῖν τὸν νόμον.
Hatred of Jesus evades the commandment of the law
(vii.50 f.). When the Jews want to serve God by perse-
cuting the disciples, they do so because they know
neither the Father nor Jesus (xvi.3).[1]

Thus in so far as Jesus as the Son and Christ takes
the place in every respect of all the other mediators
and so of the Torah too, the Torah is thereby at the
same time abolished and fulfilled. The evidence of
this is that genuine listening to the law leads to faith in
Jesus and that rejection of Jesus is at the same time
rebellion against the law.

But the law is never used in John as a rule for the
Christian behaviour of the community. This is confirmed by the Johannine letters and similarly by the
Revelation of John. It is not a matter of chance
that νόμος is never found in any of these. John does
not even once bring forward the proof that when the
law of love is carried out the genuine purpose of the
law is fulfilled.

All this puts the gospel[2] into the generation and the
period after the real conflict concerning the recognition
of the law and sets it in this respect in a line with
James and Hebrews.

[1] cf. also iii.10: if Nicodemus were a true teacher in Israel,
Jesus' word would not be so incomprehensible to him.
[2] Though not necessarily the author too.

APPENDIX[1]

1. ἀνομία

THE privative prefix considered together with the content of the word νόμος gives two shades of meaning for ἀνομία. Either (a) it is a statement of fact: *there is or was no law in existence*, 'without a (the) law', or (b) the word means 'contrary to a (the) law'. In the latter case it contains at the same time a judgement, since it assumes that there is in fact a binding law. This gives to ἀνομία the meaning of *wrongdoing, sin*. Yet actually the two meanings cannot usually be at all strictly separated from each other; the emphasis alone can be shifted.

For (a) see P. Oxy. 1121.20; ἅπαντα ὡς ἐν ἀνομία(ι)ς ἀπεσύλησαν[2]; Philo *Leg. All.* 3, 79: Melchizedek is a law-abiding king, not a tyrant *the one being the author of laws, the other of lawlessness* (ἀνομία). For (b) Philo *Conf. Ling.* 108 speaks of *mob-rule* in which *injustice and lawlessness* (ἀνομία) *are paramount*. In *Ebr.* 143 ἀνομία and ἀπαιδευσία (*ignorance*) are placed side by side. This is found also in classical Greek, e.g. in Demosthenes 24.152: when a decision reached by ballot dissolves the constitution νόμῳ καινῷ, this must not be called νόμος but ἀνομία. So even if the change were made so to say legally, it can be called ἀνομία.

In this sense ἀνομία can denote a total condition of lawlessness or wickedness: Philo *Spec. Leg.* I.188: *through their new obedience they have washed away their old lawlessness* (ἀνομία). Yet ἀνομία, especially in the plural,

---

[1] For the words here discussed, cf. also the dictionaries.
[2] Preisigke's dictionary renders this: *as though there were no legal protection.*

can equally well indicate a particular act. Ps. Sol. xv.10: *Their* (i.e. the sinners') *iniquities* (ἀνομίαι) *shall pursue them unto Sheol beneath* (cf. also *Papiri Florentini* 382,49).

In the LXX ἀνομία occurs frequently, yet it has no constant Hebrew equivalent. It corresponds most often to '*awōn* (*iniquity* c. 60 times), to '*awen* (*evil* c. 25 times, especially in the Psalms), to *peša'* (*sin* c. 20 times), to *tō'ēbāh* (*abomination* c 25 times, especially in Ezekiel).[1] In the LXX ἀνομία has all the meanings stated above. It occurs frequently in the plural and in this form describes the individual deeds (e.g. Gen. xix. 15: *lest you be dismayed with the evil deeds* (ἀνομίαις) *of the city*). The state of ἀνομία is seen e.g. in Ps. xxxii. 5 (LXX xxxi.5): *I did not hide my* ἀνομία), xvii.24 *et passim*. Generally no direct reference is made to the law, or at any rate not to an essentially greater extent than is on the whole usual in the case of the OT idea of sin, which is after all naturally brought into line with the commandments of God. So it is of course natural that ἀνομία becomes one of the main terms for sin. Growing standardisation and colourlessness here go together.

In the NT ἀνομία has the same range as elsewhere. In the plural (only in quotations), it means the simple *sinful act*; in this connexion no thought is given to its association with the law as the yardstick by which the deed in question is shown to be a sin (Rom. iv.7; Heb. x.17; so too in a variant reading in Heb. viii.12). In Titus ii.14 (a quotation) ἀπὸ πάσης ἀνομίας must be understood less definitely as a general condition because it is contrasted with ζηλωτὴς καλῶν ἔργων.

In Rom. vi.19 ἀνομία as a single act occurs beside ἀνομία for the general condition of being alienated from the law brought about by such acts, though this is

1 Besides these it corresponds to about 20 other Hebrew words, but only once to most of these.

understood not as a statement but as a judgement. Service to sin leads to a general condition of ἀνομία. Similarly (in an antithesis) we find in Heb. i.9 (a quotation): ἠγάπησας δικαιοσύνην καὶ ἐμίσησας ἀνομίαν and analogous to this in II Cor. vi.14: δικαιοσύνη and ἀνομία are mutually exclusive, like faith and unbelief, Christ and Belial. Since Paul is speaking here to a Christian community which is not tied to the standard of the OT law, it is evident that here ἀνομία does not derive its chief meaning from the OT, but means simply sin, unrighteousness. The same holds good for ἄνθρωπος τῆς ἀνομίας in II Thess. ii.3. Verse 4 depicts what are the consequences of ἀνομία. It is true that this behaviour is also contrary to the commandment of the OT, but the judgement expressed here is both more explicit and more general, and ἀνομία has in fact no meaning other than that of ἁμαρτία which is a reading found in some texts. The same is true of μυστήριον τῆς ἀνομίας in verse 7. The expression ἀποστασία in verse 3 is of primary significance for the description which follows.

In Matthew ἀνομία may allude more definitely to the law and its violation; at least this is likely in Matt. xxiii.28 where it is said particularly to those practising legal piety ἔσωθεν δὲ ἐστε μεστοὶ ὑποκρίσεως καὶ ἀνομίας. There is a less close connexion with the law in Matt. vii.23, xiii.41 (both are quotations) and in xxiv.12.

I John iii.4: πᾶς ὁ ποιῶν τὴν ἁμαρτίαν καὶ τὴν ἀνομίαν ποιεῖ, καὶ ἡ ἁμαρτία ἐστὶν ἡ ἀνομία is not completely clear. The obvious explanation is no doubt: if a man does ἁμαρτία his action is at the same time judged to be ἀνομία. In that case the meaning of ἁμαρτία would be more or less fixed and defined (hence the article: τήν); the sentence would be aimed at people who perhaps say: The ἁμαρτία if it exists is not serious. It cannot be held against one who has made a true confession, the

spiritual man. But if ἀνομία contains thus for readers
and the writer a derogatory verdict which ἁμαρτία
apparently did not have for every one without qualifi-
cation, then this can hardly be due in I John to a
reference to the OT law inherent in the word.[1] On
the contrary ἀνομία can have its own emphasis even
with a more general meaning, which would amount
more or less to *rebellion against, resistance to* God, *estrange-
ment from* God, and this would be supported by verses
6b, 9 f. Then a free translation of iii.4 would be
roughly: *everyone who commits sin is thereby in a state of
rebellion against God, indeed sin is nothing but revolt against
God*.

Yet it may be asked whether it would not also be
possible to assume νόμος in the sense understood by
Christians, for whom the command to love God and
one's neighbour means the law of Christ and so 'the
law' in its real sense. The allusion to the achievement
of Jesus in verse 5 and especially in verse 11 could
support this.[2]

2. ἄνομος

Concerning ἄνομος *having no law* essentially the same

[1] If the passage is to be understood as a clear repudiation of
antinomianism (thus Windisch, *Die Katholischen Briefe* ([2]1930,
[3]1951), *ad loc.*) then the sentence must be automatically inverted
and understood as 'ἀνομία is ἁμαρτία', and this is not possible
because of the first part of the verse.

[2] It will hardly be practicable to think of so distinguishing
ἁμαρτία and ἀνομία in meaning that ἀνομία as a sin against the law
would at the same time be a sin against one's neighbour, whilst
ἁμαρτία would be sin against God, (or even the other way round
with a corresponding alteration in the sense). In that case the
sentence would be directed against a separation of the two by
saying that sin against God includes also the violation of the
command which directs me to my neighbour (thus e.g. also
H. H. Wendt, *Die Johannesbriefe und das johanneische Christentum*
(1925), pp. 60 f.

may be said as concerning ἀνομία which is derived from it. The emphasis can be laid (*a*) on the objective fact that *a or the law does not exist* (which naturally is rare, since in general there are laws everywhere; but cf. e.g. Plat. *Polit.* 302e); or (*b*), and this is the usual meaning, on the subjective attitude, i.e. *paying no regard to the (existing) law, behaving as if there were no law(s)*. Since other people as a rule regard this as wrong, this involves expressing a judgement. In this case ἄνομος easily acquires the more general sense of *unrighteous*, with no strict allusion to a particular law.

In Judaism ὁ ἄνομος or οἱ ἄνομοι often denote the Gentiles. Here it is difficult to distinguish where this only states that they do not have the law or where it passes judgement on them as sinners. Usually the latter view seems to prevail. In Ps. Sol. xvii.18: *Over the whole earth were they scattered by lawless men* (ὑπὸ ἀνόμων). It is said of Pompey in Ps. Sol. xvii.11: *The lawless one* (ὁ ἄνομος) *laid waste our land*. Here ἄνομος has the more general meaning of *evil-doer*. In the LXX ἄνομος occurs about 30 times for reša' (*wicked*) and in other places too for more than 25 Hebrew equivalents, mostly indeed only once each. There can be no exact Hebrew equivalent in this case any more than in that of ἀνομία, if only for the reason that there is no privative prefix in Hebrew.

In the New Testament ἄνομος is used occasionally simply to state a fact. When in Rom. ii.12 ἀνόμως ἁμαρτάνειν and ἐν νόμῳ ἁμαρτάνειν are placed side by side, the former means simply that the sin was committed without knowledge of the law. Similarly the ἄνομοι of I Cor. ix.21 to whom Paul accommodates himself are distinguished from those who are ὑπὸ νόμου by the fact that they are actually ignorant of the law and are not aware of any obligation to it. οἱ ἄνομοι also occurs in a weaker sense in Luke xxii.37 (quotation), and also in a variant reading in Mark xv.28 and in Acts ii.23 (here for the Gentiles).

But I Cor. ix.21 in particular shows how definitely the meaning of ἄνομος nevertheless includes a judgement. For Paul immediately takes steps to counter a very obvious misunderstanding by saying that he was to these ἄνομοι indeed ὡς ἄνομος but that he was not on that account ἄνομος θεοῦ (cf. ἔννομος below).

If ἄνομος is intended to convey a judgement, it does not always even in the New Testament refer to the law in particular, but has a more general meaning. Thus clearly in I Tim. i.9: δικαίῳ νόμος οὐ κεῖται, ἀνόμοις δὲ καὶ ἀνυποτάκτοις. Ἄνομοι are simply people who behave wickedly. It is not implied in this expression, though it is in the whole sentence, that this is something condemned by the law.[1] Similarly in a general sense in II Peter ii.8: *the people of Sodom vex Lot* ἀνόμοις ἔργοις, *by their wicked doings*. II Thess. ii.8 should not be rendered by, for example, 'transgressor of the law' but simply by 'evil-doers' (cf. ἀνομία, p. 135ff).

3. ἔννομος

ἔννομος is the counterpart of ἄνομος, but does not occur so frequently. First it means simply *according to the law, he who (or that which) remains within the law* P. Oxy. 1204.24: ἵνα ἐννομώτερον ἀκουσθείη concerning the trial which should be conducted in accordance with the law. Aeschin. *Tim.* 3.230 mentions a measure according to the law (ἔννομον), contrasted with one that is contrary to the law (παρὰ νομον). Cf. *Tim.* 1.8; Philo *Abr.* 242; *Poster. C.* 176. When applied to persons ἔννομος means *just, upright*, cf. Plat. *Resp.* IV.424e.

---

[1] Debrunner indeed considers that the sentence would have more point if the ἄνομοι were those who do not concern themselves with the laws (or the law), just as the ἀνυπότακτοι are those who do not wish to submit to it (so privately).

In Judaism ἔννομος usually refers to the OT law. In Ecclus. Prol. 14: the grandfather wrote his book in order that the readers *might make progress much more by living according to the law* (διὰ τῆς ἐννόμου βιώσεως); the grandson translates it for those people who are *fashioning their manners beforehand to live according to the law* (ἐννόμως) (35 f.). More generally in Prov. xxxi.25: (the virtuous housewife) *opens her mouth wisely and according to law.*

In the New Testament ἔννομος occurs in Acts xix.39: the ἔννομος ἐκκλησία is the lawful, legally incontestable, legally summoned assembly, as contrasted with the riotous popular gathering described just before. In I Cor. ix.21 Paul says of himself that, even though when dealing with Gentiles he sets the law aside, yet he himself is not an ἄνομος of God but ἔννομος Χριστοῦ. The latter is intended to determine the meaning of the former. Since he is ἔννομος Χριστοῦ he is not ἄνομος θεοῦ. The two genitives no doubt refer to the νόμος contained in ἄνομος and ἔννομος.[1]

4. νομικός

In classical Greek νομικός occurs only as an adjective (e.g. in Plat. *Leg.* 625a). The meaning is *according to, corresponding to, the law.*[2] Later νομικός became largely a technical term for a *lawyer*, especially a *notary*. Epict. *Diss.* II.13.6: 'If one does not know the laws of a city, one consults a νομικός'. In the papyri νομικός often occurs as a title after the name (cf. P. Oxy. 237.VIII.2 ff.).[3] But νομικός also continues to be used as an adjective (as an adverb in the

---

[1] cf. Schlatter, *Paulus, der Bote Jesu. Eine Deutung seiner Briefe an die Korinther* (¹1934, ²1956), *ad loc.*

[2] Preisigke, *Wörterbuch*, III, p. 135; Moulton-Milligan, *Vocabulary of the Greek Testament*, s.v.

[3] Examples in Preisigke, *Wörterbuch*, III, p. 135.

Letter of Aristeas 142). In Judaism the designation νομικός acquires a connexion with the OT law, cf. IV Macc. v.4: *Eleazer, a priest by birth, trained in knowledge of the law* (τὴν ἐπιστήμην νομικός).

In the New Testament νομικός is used once as an adjective, in Titus iii.9: καὶ μάχας νομικὰς περιΐστασο, *controversies, quarrels which refer to the law* (*or the OT in general*). The expression leaves it open whether it is a question of the validity of the law as a rule of life for Christians, or of theories which are to be proved from the scriptures. Since Titus i.10 mentions the party of the circumcision, the first interpretation must be considered; yet in view of the false doctrines attacked in the Pastoral Epistles the latter is the more likely.

In Matthew and Luke νομικός is sometimes used for the leaders of the Jewish people. But they are given the name only in contexts dealing with the administration or the understanding of the law. In Matt. xxii.35 (parallel Luke x.25), the question about the most important commandment is put by a νομικός When Mark says γραμματεύς (xii.26), the meaning is the same, but judging according to the context νομικός is more appropriate.[1]

In Luke vii.30 too νομικός will have been chosen intentionally just because βουλὴ τοῦ θεοῦ here has John the Baptist in view, not the law. Those who wish and ought to concern themselves with the law in a special manner do not concern themselves with the purpose of God now being made known. In Luke xi.45 f., 52 νομικός is evidently intended to underline what are the burdens in question here and how the locking up is done. Luke xiv.3 is also concerned with the understanding of the law.

[1] Since Mark is writing for Romans, νομικός is ambiguous owing to the technical meaning of the word already mentioned. Hence the word is lacking in Mark altogether.

It is hardly possible to decide conclusively what is the meaning of νομικός in Titus iii.13; but since Zenas is not included amongst the opponents and the addition of νομικός as a title after a name is in common use elsewhere, the more probable interpretation is *lawyer* or *notary*.[1]

5. νόμιμος

νόμιμος usually means *conformable to the rule, to the regulation, to what is right*.[2] It is used in P. Oxy. 1201.18: of lots; in Chr. II.372.13 (Preisigke, *Wörterbuch*, s.v.): of a legally valid marriage, cf. Epict. III.10.8. Used as a noun τὸ νόμιμον is that which is fair and reasonable.[3]

In the LXX νόμιμος occurs only once as an adjective: II Macc. iv.11 in the sense of *lawful*; elsewhere τὸ νόμιμον or τὰ νόμιμα are the translation of ḥōq, ḥuqqāh (*statute*), tōrāh. This usage probably assumes that there are only, so far as the law is concerned, individual regulations and rules, so that τὸ νόμιμον means something like 'legal rules'.

In the New Testament νόμιμος occurs only as an adverb: I Tim. i.8; II Tim. ii.5. In the case of II Tim. ii.8 it is evident that νομίμως does not mean 'in conformity with the OT law', but using the metaphorical language of the contest either with the special meaning *according to the rules of the contest*[4], *in the appropriate manner*, or in a general sense: *well done, efficiently*.

In I Tim. i.8 νομίμως will not mean: corresponding to the OT law,[5] but simply *in the appropriate way*,[6] although owing to the context the two are completely

---

[1] cf. Dibelius, *Die Pastoralbriefe* (³1955), *ad loc.*

[2] The word was formed at a time when νόμος did not yet mean 'law' (Debrunner).

[3] cf. Preisigke, *Wörterbuch*, s.v.; also Philo *Decal.* 37, *Abr.* 276.

[4] cf. Wohlenberg, *Die Pastoralbriefe* (³1923), *ad loc.*

[5] cf. Wohlenberg, *Die Pastoralbriefe*, *ad loc.*

[6] Wohlenberg and Dibelius, *ad loc.*

synonymous here. At any rate the proper use of the law is different from that made by those who pretend to be teachers of the law.

6. νομοθέτης

νομοθέτης means *lawgiver* (cf. Aristot. *Pol.* II.12 p. 1274a 31 f., *ib.* II.6 p. 1265a 18 ff., Diod. S. 12.11.3, Philo *Spec. Leg.* IV.120). In Judaism Moses is in a special sense a νομοθέτης (thus in e.g. Letter of Aristeas 131, 148, 312); so is God (Philo *Sacr. AC* 131: God is *Himself the lawgiver and fountain of laws*). In the LXX the only passage with νομοθέτης, in Ps. ix.21 (EVV 20), depends on the *K^ethib mōreh* (*teacher*) instead of the *Q^ere mōrā'* (*fear*).

In the New Testament it occurs only in James iv.12. The meaning of the preceding sentence must govern the meaning of the title νομοθέτης for God in this passage and cannot itself be determined by this[1] (cf. p. 128).

7. νομοθεσία

νομοθεσία (derived from νομοθέτης) usually no longer suggests the act of legislation, but what has come out of the act, hence according to the context, the *law*, the *constitution*, and also the *code of laws*. Hence in a Jewish context, parallel to νόμος, it quite simply denotes the Pentateuch (cf. Diod. S. 12.11.4: P. Oxy. 1119.18). In the LXX only in II Macc. vi.23: Eleazar is determined to remain steadfast owing to the *holy God-given law* (θεόκτιστος νομοθεσία). In the Letter of Aristeas 15 the νομοθεσία of the Jews is to be translated. In Philo even the unwritten law can be described

---

[1] Barnabas xxi.4: *Be good lawgivers one to another*, is interesting too. Verse 5 shows that this is not used in the sense of allowing complete freedom. But this usage shows the wide range which the word can have.

as ἄγραφος νομοθεσία (*Abr.* 5); elsewhere in his books too νομοθεσία is often the Pentateuch: *Cher.* 87: πολλαχοῦ τῆς νομοθεσίας = in many passages of the Pentateuch.

It is true that occasionally the meaning of legislation is nearer, for instance in Philo *Vit. Mos.* 2.2: one of the faculties of Moses is concerned with lawgiving (cf. also Ditt. Or. 326.26). Here the act of legislation can at any rate be in mind. Similarly also no doubt in Plat. *Leg.* III.684e.

In the only passage where νομοθεσία occurs in the New Testament, Rom. ix.4, the most natural meaning is 'law' and not legislation in particular. It is not the act of legislation which is named as one of the prerogatives of Israel, but the actual possession of the law (cf. Rom. iii.1 f.).

8. νομοθετέω

νομοθετεῖν (derived from νομοθέτης) means (*a*) *to be active as a legislator, to frame laws*; so Plat. *Polit.* 294c; Letter of Aristeas 240. The recipient of the laws is in the dative, or in the accusative, cf. Philo *Poster. C.* 143. (*b*) *to ordain a thing by law, to settle by law*: cf. Letter of Aristeas 144. Both meanings can appear in the passive, cf. Plat. *Leg.* III.701d. The passive is more frequent where *things are ordained by law*, e.g. Philo *Vit. Mos.* II.218, P. Oxy. 1119.24.

Compared with this the LXX has no special usage; it must merely be stated that when the word is used a strict reference to the Mosaic law need not always be associated with it (cf. Ps. xxvi.11, where νομοθετεῖν almost means *to instruct* (Hebrew *yārāh* in the *hiph'il*).

The two New Testament passages reflect both these main meanings. In Heb. vii.11 νομοθετεῖν is used in the passive of persons to whom the law is given. What it is intended to describe more precisely (whether it is to be rendered as 'the law' or 'law') is decided not by the word νομοθετεῖν, but by the context, as well as by the interpretation of ἐπ᾽ αὐτῆς. ἐπί with the genitive as denoting the object in respect of which the law is given does not occur elsewhere with νομοθετεῖν (yet it does with περί in II Macc. iii.15, Philo Vit. Mos. II.218). Since moreover the meaning of the interpolated sentence would otherwise be rather thin, it is probably a question of the whole law, and not of the law regulating the cult in particular. In Heb. viii.6 the relative clause can refer to λειτουργία or to διαθήκη; this is immaterial as regards its meaning, yet the expression seems to suit λειτουργία better. In any case the new thing in question is established, ordained. The νόμος included in νομοθετεῖν must therefore be understood in a more general sense and not as referring to the OT.

9. παρανομία

(a) παρανομία denotes in classical Greek, as in later Greek, a general condition, (which of course shows itself in individual acts also). Ps. Sol. xvii.20: *The king was a transgressor* (ἐν παρανομίᾳ), *and the judge was disobedient* (ἐν ἀπαθείᾳ) *and the people sinful* (ἐν ἁμαρτίᾳ). In the LXX παρανομία is infrequent (nine times) and has no constant Hebrew equivalent. παράνομος occurs more often. As in the case of ἀνομία the distinctions made in the original language are blurred. In παρανομία too the connexion with the standard of the law, which underlies the word, is no longer clearly maintained. In the passage cited from the Ps. Sol., παρανομία does not refer to the law any more than do ἀπείθεια or ἁμαρτία, although of course on the other hand in Judaism the law is the norm or criterion for all such judgements. (b) παρανομία also means the *single unjust action*; thus e.g. in Philo Vit. Mos. 1, 295: Balaam advises Balak *that the one way by which the Hebrews could be overthrown was disobedience* (παρανομία); cf. P. Oxy. 1119.18, where παρανομία against the imperial orders must be punished.

In the New Testament the only passage with παρανομία is II Peter ii.16: Balaam ἔλεγξιν ἔσχεν ἰδίας παρανομίας. As regards verse 16b, either it is a concessive clause: 'although . . . restrained him'; in that case ἔλεγξις has the meaning of punishment and the παρανομία is his promise to curse Israel for gain. Or verse 16b describes what ἔλεγξιν ἔσθεν involved. ἔλεγξις would then be the conviction preceding the act, and thus a warning, and the παρανομία would consist in the intention to curse Israel. The difference has no significance at all for παρανομία. But the question influences the meaning of the whole passage. Either the sentence means that the false teachers too refuse to accept any warning, or that, if they will not accept a warning, they will be punished like Balaam who ignored the warning. In any case παρανομία is a *wrong action*, without any direct reference to the law being implied.

10. παρανομέω

παρανομέω means to *transgress a law, an ordinance that has been laid down*. Cf. Dittenberger, *Sylloge Inscriptionum Graecarum* ([3]1915-24), 218, 21 f.: οἱ παρανομοῦντες are people who violate a particular ordinance. In Plat. *Resp.* I.338e: Let that which is serviceable to the ruling class be the law everywhere and let those who infringe it be punished ὡς παρανομοῦντά τε καὶ ἀδικοῦντα But παρανομεῖν has often a more general meaning: *to offend*; in Ps. Sol. xvi.8: *let not the beauty of an ungodly* (παρανομούσης), *woman beguile me*. In the LXX it occurs only five times, with a different Hebrew equivalent on each occasion; e.g. in Ps. lxxiv.5 (EVV lxxv.4) it is parallel to ἁμαρτάνειν. In the passive παρανομεῖν can also be used of a person.[1]

---

[1] cf. P. Greci e Latini (= P. Soc.) 330.8 cf. Preisigke, *Worterbuch* s.v.

In the New Testament it occurs only in Acts xxiii.3: σὺ κάθη κρίνων με κατὰ τὸν νόμον, καὶ παρανομῶν κελεύεις με τύπτεσθαι. Here the contrast with κατὰ τὸν νόμον makes παρανομεῖν mean specifically the *violation of the law* and it is probably not merely a general expression for doing wrong.

INDEX OF REFERENCES

RABBINIC

(B *or* J *indicates Babylonian or Jerusalem Talmud*)

Talmud and Midrash

GENERAL INDEX